PENGUIN BOOKS

IMPERIAL CHINA

Charis Chan is a freelance journalist, specializing in Chinese history and arts. She graduated in Oriental Studies at Oxford in 1978 and then obtained a diploma in Chinese history at Nankai University. She went on to live in Hong Kong for three years, where she worked as an editor, before returning to London. Her first book, the *Collins Illustrated Guide to All China*, was published in 1988. She is currently living in Oxford and preparing for a Ph.D. thesis on contemporary Chinese art.

Other titles in the series:
CLASSICAL TURKEY
ISLAMIC SPAIN
MUGHAL INDIA
THE ROAD TO SANTIAGO DE COMPOSTELA

In preparation:
ANCIENT EGYPT
CHÂTEAUX OF THE LOIRE
MEDIEVAL TUSCANY AND UMBRIA

IMPERIAL CHINA

CHARIS CHAN

PENGUIN BOOKS

PENGUIN BOOKS

Published by the Penguin Group
Penguin Books Ltd, 27 Wrights Lane, London W8 5TZ, England
Viking Penguin, a division of Penguin Books USA Inc.
375 Hudson Street, New York, New York 10014, USA
Penguin Books Australia Ltd, Ringwood, Victoria, Australia
Penguin Books Canada Ltd, 2801 John Street, Markham, Ontario, Canada L3R 1B4
Penguin Books (NZ) Ltd, 182–190 Wairau Road, Auckland 10, New Zealand

Penguin Books Ltd, Registered Offices: Harmondsworth, Middlesex, England

Designed and produced by Johnson Editions Ltd
15 Grafton Square, London SW4 0DQ

First published in Great Britain by Viking 1991
Published in Penguin Books 1992
10 9 8 7 6 5 4 3 2 1

Series conceived by Georgina Harding
Senior Editor: Valerie Bingham
Editor: Bridget Harney
Series design: Clare Finlaison
Design: Wendy Bann
Maps and plans: David Woodroffe
Picture research: Emma Milne
Index: Hilary Bird

Typesetting: DP Photosetting, Aylesbury, Bucks
Origination: Fotographics, London-Hong Kong
Printed in Italy by Rotolito Lombarda Spa, Milan

CONTENTS

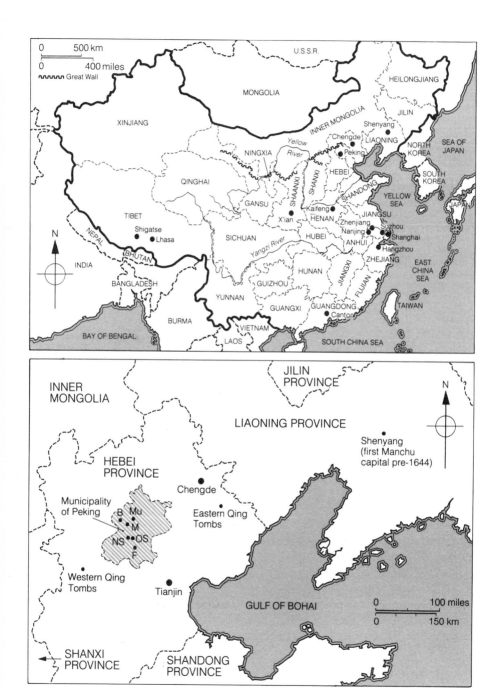

FOREWORD

A book on the architecture of imperial China inevitably demands that the reader grapple with a host of strange names and concepts. Not least are the confusing chronologies. In order to make the text easier to follow without too much need to refer to the chronological chart at the back of the book, the dates of dynasties and the reigns of emperors are given when they first occur in each new chapter. (Until 1911, the Chinese calculated their dates using a lunar calendar, the lunar new year starting one to two months later than the solar new year.)

One important note to bear in mind is that in this book the date of a building is given as the time when it was completed in its initial phase. Work on the building may have commenced many years before this date and, moreover, the building may have been renovated or added to at later periods. In many cases, the year given for the building of a hall or a temple does not indicate the period from which the present structure dates. An interesting example of this problem is the buildings of the Ming Tombs, many of which were damaged in the early years of the Qing dynasty and were restored by order of the Qian Long emperor in the 18th century out of respect for his imperial predecessors.

The names of the emperors are also problematic. We usually refer to Chinese emperors by their reign titles, i.e. the title of the period of time given to their rule. The Chinese emperors had personal names and, after their death, were also given ancestral or temple names which were used during sacrifices to their spirits. So, for example, the Qian Long emperor, who ruled from 1736–1795, had the personal name of Hong Li; after his death he was given the temple name of Gao Zong, High Ancestor, and the posthumous title of Emperor Chun. All this can be very confusing, so I have deemed it easier to call the emperors by their reign title rather than by their personal or ancestral names. Books on Chinese history tend to be inconsistent — calling the earlier Tang emperors by their temple names and the Ming and Qing emperors by their reign

(Opposite — top)
Map of China.

(Opposite — bottom)
Map of Hebei Province in China, showing sites covered in the book
F Forbidden City;
NS New Summer Palace, *Yi He Yuan*;
OS Old Summer Palace, *Yuan Ming Yuan*;
M Ming Tombs;
B Ba Da Ling section of Great Wall;
Mu Mu Tian Yu section of Great Wall.

titles. This is because of the western familiarity with the reign titles by which Ming and Qing porcelain is dated.

Because of limited space, with apologies, religious architecture and its decorative motifs have been treated in much less depth than the residential, garden and ceremonial buildings of the emperors. Religion was an important part of the lives of many of the Ming and Qing emperors, their wives and mothers. The number of temples founded and funded by members of the imperial family is legion. One of the most famous Buddhist temples in Peking, the Lama Temple, *Yong He Gong*, was originally the residence of the fourth son of the Kang Xi emperor of the Qing dynasty. This prince was to become the Yong Zheng emperor, and his son, the Qian Long emperor, later gave the mansion over to the Buddhist clergy.

This book could not have been written without the help, advice and practical assistance of many people in Britain, China and Hong Kong. My thanks go to my husband Edward Chan for all his help with our children Bart and Thomasina, T.Z. Chang for his hospitality and inspiration, Mark O'Neill and Louise do Rosario for their hospitality in Peking, Mary Tregear of the Ashmolean Museum and Tony Hyder of the Oriental Institute in Oxford, Wu Jun for his liaison work, a couple of kind taxi drivers in Peking who allowed me to take their cars down the bumpiest of tracks with no complaints, and lastly, the editors Gabrielle Townsend, Sandy Shepherd, Valerie Bingham and Bridget Harney and, Emma Milne the picture researcher.

This book is dedicated to those
who lost their lives on June 4th 1989.
1898, 1911, 1919, 1949, 1979.

PLANNING AN ITINERARY

Most tours to China, which include a stay in the capital, offer visits to the most famous monuments included in this book. The tour groups usually allow half a day at each venue and there is a well organized route through the monuments, which includes the major buidings. In the case of the Temple of Heaven, visitors see most of the buildings of the complex. But in the case of the Forbidden City, the buildings are too numerous and the distances too great to allow anything more than a fleeting glance of the palaces in half a day. Serious sightseers will need at least a full day or more to enjoy any of the major sights included in this volume.

All the monuments included here, with the exception of Chengde, are within a few hours' drive from the centre of Peking. Most can be reached by tour bus from the large hotels. However, and this is the case for all historical sites in China, it is always better to have your own transport, whether taxi or bicycle, so that you can dictate the speed and times of your visit. It is also usually cheaper in the end to make your own arrangements if you can share the cost of a hired taxi with a travelling companion. Tour visits to sights are usually expensive as they contain an obligatory luncheon at a highly inflated price. In the case of tour visits to distant sights, the package could cost you around a hundred times the price it would cost if you arranged the trip yourself and found cheap accommodation. However, the value of the pre-arranged tour is that you do not have to do all the wearisome and frustrating legwork of booking and buying the tickets.

Visitors with an extended time in Peking should, if possible, hire a bicycle for sightseeing. Local buses are always crowded, very slow and also difficult to use because of the problem of deciphering bus stops. Taxis are a good idea for the wealthier traveller, but the bicycle is the best way to go as the terrain is flat and most people in the city travel by bicycle and not by car. The bicycle gives you the true taste of local life. All the sights detailed in the Peking chapter can be visited with ease by bicycle. For those who are fit, the parks described in Chapter Two are also accessible by bicycle. The Great Wall and the Imperial Tombs can be visited within a day by tour bus or taxi.

Chengde is a four- to six-hour train ride away from Peking (the faster time is possible if you take the early morning express, the slower time is based on the late morning train). Trains are always crowded in China and tickets must be bought at least four days in advance. If you want to use the train for journeys to any of the major cities in China, it is advisable to book your tickets at least one or two weeks in advance. The main railway stations usually have a special counter where train tickets are sold to foreigners (at higher prices than those for locals) and this means that you must find out where the special counter is and not try and buy a ticket at the main counter, where, in most cases, the ticket clerks will be unable to speak to you in a foreign language.

Check with your hotel reception before planning a major journey outside the capital. Once outside the capital, you will find the system of returning to it slightly more problematic and arcane than the system of leaving. Return tickets do not exist on planes or trains in China — it is just too complicated. Most railway stations have complex regulations on when certain tickets can be sold before the journey. For example, when you want to leave Chengde, you have to buy a ticket to go back to Peking one day before you leave. The Chengde booking office will not accept a booking any further in advance than 24 hours. This is because Chengde has a small railway station and cannot cope with the complications of advance booking. Do not ever think it is possible to just turn up and hop on a train — that is unless you want to travel standing up with the pigs and chickens!

The decision of when to travel to China should be made on the basis of how far you are travelling within China and how fit you are. The winter months in the north of China and in the high altitudes of Tibet, make it an unattractive season for travel except for the most hardy. The high summer temperatures experienced throughout all of China should be taken into account if you do not like hot weather and high humidity. The combination of heat and humidity is quite exhausting if you are planning to travel over long distances. Spring and summer are the mildest seasons, but if most of your stay is planned in

south China, which experiences mild winters, it is advisable to travel off-season.

The Hall of Supreme Harmony set on a three-tiered terrace known as a dragon pavement, the Forbidden City.

If you are planning to visit China, then it is worth taking into account the diversity of landscapes and architecture found in north and south China. This book does not deal with the architecture of the south, but it would be a shame for visitors to the country to miss out on the wonderful temples and gardens found in the south and southeast. It is probably only possible to visit all the sights listed in the various chapters of this book if you are likley to be visiting Peking for an extended period. Although I lived in China for more than a year, I managed to see so many places only because I have been going back to Peking regularly over 10 years. There are many monuments which I have yet to see. I hope that this volume helps to bring pleasure to your walks and bicycle rides round the landmarks of Chinese imperial architecture.

NOTE ON PRONUNCIATION

The Chinese language uses ideographs and does not have an alphabet or phonetic pronunciation system. All ideographs have a sound and tone value which can vary from region to region in China. The sound value known as 'Mandarin' or 'Putonghua' is the pronunciation of the capital region of China. In order to learn Chinese or write the sound of an ideograph in the Roman alphabet, systems of romanization have evolved. The most widespread romanization system was the 19th-century version known as Wade-Giles, which gave us such words as 'Ching' dynasty. The romanization system in current usage in the People's Republic China, and used in this book, is known as 'Pinyin', and has some unusual ways of romanizing consonant values. Thus the 'Ching' dynasty of the Wade-Giles system is written as 'Qing' in the Pinyin method. The sound denoted by 'q' is the same as the 'ch"' of the Wade-Giles system; 'x' in the Pinyin system was denoted as 'hs' in Wade-Giles; 'c' in the Pinyin was 'ts"' in Wade-Giles; 'z' in the Pinyin was 'ts' in Wade-Giles. The sound values are an approximation as the mouth position is different in pronouncing the consonants. As a rough guide to Pinyin pronunciation:

q   has the equivalent sound of 'ch' as in '*ch*ew', but with the mouth rounder and more open.

x   is the same sound as '*sh*oot' with the mouth held narrow and pulled back as in a smile.

c   is the equivalent of a *ts* pronounced together with great emphasis and teeth close together.

z   is the equivalent of *ts*, pronounced more softly with the teeth wider apart and the tongue held against the teeth.

INTRODUCTION

The imperial epoch in China lasted an astonishing 2,132 years from 221 BC until 1911, when the last boy emperor was overthrown by a small military uprising in central China, news of which spread along the telegraph wires and sparked rebellion throughout the country. An institution which began with the value systems of a late Bronze-age society was to last into our era of accelerated technological change — change that was to play a major part in undermining and finally destroying the ancient imperial order. Yet, even at the beginning of this century, the emperor ran his court and performed his ceremonial duties in a palace compound designed according to the prescriptions of pre-imperial, classical texts of the Bronze-age **Zhou dynasty** (1122–221 BC). The palace buildings themselves may date from only the 14th to 19th centuries, but the principles of their layout and functions were based on interpretations and reinterpretations of those early documents

A Bronze-Age tripod of the Zhou dynasty (c. 1122–221 BC).

on imperial ritual and the esoteric art of geomancy — a form of divination used for the auspicious siting of buildings. Until the last emperor abdicated in 1912, his environment, as much as his duties, was shaped by ideas over two thousand years old.

It is thus surprising to realize that China, a civilization as ancient and glorious as the Egypt of the pharaohs, has no surviving monuments contemporaneous with the pyramids of

A look-out tower on the Great Wall, at Ba Da Ling, dating from the Ming dynasty.

Egypt. Those parts of the Great Wall that were built in the first millenium BC, now stand as broken earth ridges in the wind-scoured deserts in the north-west of the country, and the sections of the Wall which most visitors see today, with their crenellated battlements and look-out towers, date from the **Ming dynasty** (1368–1644). Only a mere half-dozen or so buildings survive from even the end of the first millenium AD, and only just over two score buildings dating from the 10th to the mid-14th century still stand.

The small number of surviving ancient buildings is attributable to the impermanent materials with which the Chinese loved to build. Stone and bricks may have been used for defensive walls and gates, highways, bridges, stupas (Buddhist relic towers) and the chambers of underground tombs, but for their palaces, houses and temples, builders worked with wood, ceramic tiles, lacquer, plaster and paint over platforms of compacted earth, bricks, or, in the case of grand buildings, raised earth terraces covered with stone slabs. The great scholar of Chinese civilization, Joseph Needham, notes with respect that the Chinese people had little desire to dominate posterity and built in a style of 'sober humanism'.

Of the fabled palaces and pleasure parks of the early dynasties, especially those of the **Han** and **Tang**, (206 BC–AD 220 and AD 618–907 respectively), eras famous for their cultural achievements, nothing remains beyond the outline of foundations. However, we can imagine their splendour from reading some of the poetry written to celebrate these imperial buildings. A form of poetry from the Han dynasty, known as *fu*, specialized in rich descriptions of architecture, giving us some idea of how important lavish buildings were in the cultural life of the ruling elite.

The building of sumptuous palaces did not go unopposed, however. Many Confucian scholars throughout Chinese history took a highly moral stand on the duties of the emperor and criticized lavish palace building programmes, denouncing them on the grounds that they wasted money, which could be better spent on good administration, and caused hardship to ordinary people who were taken away from the land to be labourers. For the Confucian moralist, a profligate emperor was a bad emperor and a bad emperor could lose the throne for his dynasty. Luckily for us, this kind of moral criticism was often ignored! Lavish architecture continued to be built, and some survived, particularly from the Ming and **Qing** (1644–1912) dynasties whose emperors did not hesitate in spending money on splendid, stylish and ornate buildings and tombs.

Because no imperial architecture survives from the period before the Ming dynasty, save for the underground vaults and stone Spirit Avenues of imperial tombs, this book is, by default, a guide to buildings of the 14th to the late 19th century. Imperial architecture is defined as the residences, official halls, pleasure parks, temples, tombs and altars of the imperial family and court. Ming and Qing emperors were often active sponsors of religious establishments — Daoist, as well as Buddhist — beyond the confines of their palaces. However, these temples have not been included in this guide as the religious architecture of China is a vast and complex field and well deserves a separate volume. Where temples are part of an imperial compound or an element in the design of the landscape of a pleasure park, they have been included.

Likewise, this guide does not explore in depth the subject of garden architecture and landscaping: gardens and their buildings are looked at in the context of the vast imperial pleasure parks and hunting grounds that were designed and maintained for the emperors as a pleasant retreat in the hot summer months. The two most famous Qing emperors, **Kang Xi** and **Qian Long** (reigned 1662–1722 and 1736–95 respectively), who liked to travel, and who frequently made extended visits to the scenic cities of central and eastern China, were keen patrons of landscape architecture both in their own pleasure palaces and in cities they visited. Many of the kiosks and viewing verandahs around the picturesque West Lake of Hangzhou, in the south-eastern province of Zhejiang, for example, were built by order of the visiting emperors. The intimate and highly stylized vistas of small private gardens were the creation of scholars and artists. Emperors often liked to include small-scale replicas of these gardens as a feature of their grander imperial resorts.

Domestic architecture, another fascinating field to explore when looking at some of the old quarters of Chinese cities, is also outside the domain of this book. Yet, in describing the principles of Chinese architecture, this guide should help the traveller enjoy and appreciate many buildings not featured in the following pages. For the Chinese family house has traditionally been built according to the same rules of layout and scale as an imperial palace. The buildings may be smaller, there may be no or meagre decoration, but the principles of design are usually identical.

Throughout Chinese history, palaces have been converted into temples, and temples into government offices or schools. When the Communists came to power in 1949 and subsequently closed temples and converted the buildings to schools, or sometimes, more insensitively, into army barracks, they were acting well within the tradition of flexible building usage (and also within the occasional tradition of religious persecution when it came to using some temples as target practice for the artillery!). Chinese buildings, except for some of the grander throne halls and ancestral tablet halls of the imperial tombs, were built to a very human and intimate scale, and this has allowed them to be transformed with ease. Chinese architecture has no equivalent of Versailles — a single building with a multitude of rooms.

A portrait of the Qing dynasty Kang Xi emperor.

Cosmic Order, Geomancy and Imperial Architecture

> If the ruler is correct, then the primal pneuma (*qi*) will be harmonious and compliant, winds and rain will be timely, auspicious stars will appear, and the yellow dragon will descend. If the ruler is not correct, then above a (strangely) transformed heaven and (below) rebellious acts will appear at the same time. (Translation of part of a text by a Han dynasty philosopher Dong Zhong Shu.)

> The boundaries of every square inch correspond to the celestial divisions on high. The (relation between the) phenomena in the heavens and the aspect (i.e. the physical features) of the earth can thus be brilliantly seen. (Translation of part of the preface to a Tang dynasty geographical work *Di Zhi Tu* by the government official Lü Wen.)

In the thousand years between the lives of the second-century BC scholar Dong Zhong Shu and the ninth-century government official, Lü Wen, there were momentous changes in the

5

political, social and religious life of imperial China. But one deeply embedded element in the core of Chinese tradition remained, not entirely untouched by political and scholarly debate but certainly little changed, and this was the belief in correlative cosmology and the central role of the emperor as the 'Son of Heaven'.

Cosmology: Order in Heaven and on Earth

Correlative cosmology can be seen as a philosophical or quasi-religious system where cosmic or natural phenomena are linked with the world of men in a relationship of significant interaction. For example, should a disaster such as an earthquake occur or the harvest fail, then the emperor could be criticized by his officials for offending Heaven. Astronomical phenomena were also closely studied for good and bad portents; this has meant that China has the longest tradition in the world of recorded celestial observations. The fixing of the calendar was very important, too, for the maintenance of good government: in an agricultural society, the ruler's ability to predict the seasons for sowing and harvesting were a symbol of his divine authority. Because it was believed that the cosmos could be disturbed by disorder on earth, even the earliest rulers had court astronomers to draw up the calendar. As far back as the **Shang dynasty** (1480–1050 BC), the royal astronomers were able to draw up an accurate lunar calendar with an intercalary month in order to take account of the discrepancy between the lunar and solar cycles. The relationship between ruler and cosmos was vital and led to the emergence of the idea that the sovereign reported to and was answerable to Heaven.

The doctrines of the 'Son of Heaven' and the 'Mandate of Heaven' were conceived during the reigns of the founding rulers of the Zhou dynasty in the 11th century BC. The sovereign as the Son of Heaven was deemed to be responsible for harmony and good government, and was accountable to Heaven, but he himself was not divine. It was the position itself that was divine. If he was inadequate for the task, then, by the Mandate of Heaven he could be removed. The early Zhou kings created these concepts in order to justify their own overthrow of the preceding Shang royal house. The idea that a ruler who was corrupt and inadequate could, with all justice, be deposed because he had 'lost' the Mandate of Heaven remained a central and potentially revolutionary tenet in the imperial creed.

The Mandate of Heaven could even accommodate the defeat of a native or 'Han' Chinese dynasty by a foreign enemy. The Manchu warriors who defeated the Chinese Ming house in 1644, and founded the Qing dynasty, were well aware of this cornerstone of Confucian philosophy. Prior to their victory, the Manchu leaders had made great efforts to master the Chinese language, study the Confucian classics and recruit disaffected Han Chinese scholars as officials in preparation for accepting the Mandate of Heaven.

The Evolution of State Religion and Ritual

In the pre-Zhou period, Heaven was not the central element in religious ritual. Instead, the Shang rulers worshipped a divine lord called Shang Di, made offerings to the souls of their ancestors, and consulted the spirits of the natural world through divination. This was a mix of theism and pantheism in which the spirits of gods as well as ancestors, the wind, rain or rivers were invoked in the interests of man. To this day, these ancient cults of ancestor worship and pantheism have remained important elements of Chinese religious practice and can still be observed in the household and temple rituals of such ultra-modern societies as Hong Kong and Singapore. When the Zhou rulers succeeded the Shang, they added the cult of Heaven to this rich mixture of spirit worship. However, in contrast to the Shang deities, Heaven was regarded as an animate but abstract cosmic force which reflected and responded to the events of the world. It was not in any way like the Hebraic or Hellenic concepts of a realm overseen by one omnipotent god or by anthropomorphic deities. The Zhou rulers added the cult of Heaven to an already rich mixture of spirit and nature worship, and from it grew an imperial state religion which was to survive in the rituals and sacrifices of emperors until the overthrow of the Qing dynasty in 1911.

The creation of a state imperial religion through the synthesis of ancient cults, Confucian philosophy and the later works of Han dynasty philosophers such as Dong Zhong Shu demanded that the Son of Heaven lead a life of complex ritual in addition to his fulfillment of administrative duties. Ritual was such an important aspect of the emperor's life that it determined how he dressed through the seasons and for ceremonies, how he ate, and even how he regulated his sex life. Ancient texts of the Zhou dynasty such as the *Yue Ling*, the Monthly Ordinances of the *Li Ji*, the 'Record of Rites', were comprehensive in their prescriptions for the ruler's lifestyle. Not only did the emperor's clothes, ceremonies and sacrifices have to conform to cosmic order, but also so did his dwellings. From very early in Chinese history, there has existed a concept that the plan or the form of a building had to conform to cosmic patterns in order to attune the workings of the imperial administration to the Will of Heaven. This concept has remained an important theme in the creation of all ceremonial architecture for the emperor.

The Science of Geomancy

It is perhaps quite logical that a culture which worshipped the spirits of mountains and rivers should have seen the landscape as alive with cosmic currents or *qi*. Out of this sense of a cosmically alive landscape came the belief in *feng shui*, or topographical divination. Meaning literally 'wind and water', it was an ancient form of geomancy based on the idea that the shape of land forms, soil types, and the configuration of watercourses could correspond with the constellations and also hold innate and changing 'auspicious' or 'inauspicious' qualities. The early origins of this practice are obscure but there are references to geomancers in the histories of the Han dynasty. By the end of the 19th century, when westerners in China had started to write studies on the subject, geomancy had become an elaborate 'science' and a major industry in the siting of houses and graves. The court and the common people largely lived and were buried by its tenets.

But the demands and considerations of court ritual and burials did not mean that all emperors accepted geomancy uncritically. We know from recorded incidents that such different emperors as the clever but wilful 16th-century Ming emperor **Wan Li** (reigned 1573–1620), who withdrew from government, and the able and energetic 17th-century Qing emperor Kang Xi (reigned 1662–1722) has reservations about the efficacy of *feng shui*. However, in their roles as emperor, neither of these intelligent emperors dared to overlook cosmic phenomena and thus challenge the doctrine of the Will of Heaven. It is possible that most of the emperors who did not have a superstitious nature and did not dabble in alchemy had a fairly healthy disregard for some of the excesses of geomancy but, for the sake of tradition, allowed its practitioners a role in tomb siting and palace building.

The Ming dynasty Wan Li emperor.

The principles of geomancy are far from clear; secrecy and contending schools of thought have made sure of that. Some diviners worked intuitively, looking at combinations of topographical aspects and somehow mystically responding to the landscape. Others worked with a learned set of rules and diviner's compass in order to make a set of readings. The readings were taken from the symbols spaced around the magnetic compass in a band of concentric circles. These symbols could represent such elements as the constellations, the seasons, winds, times of the day, etc. From consulting the compass, the geomancer could 'divine' the combination of auspicious or inauspicious elements at a particular site. Both

A geomancer's compass.

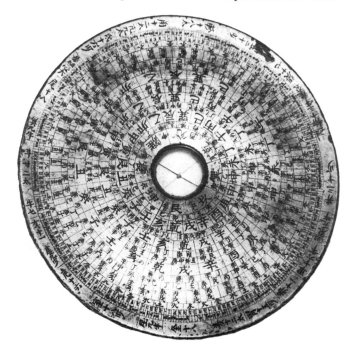

'intuitive' and 'compass' geomancers were believed to have highly valuable knowledge for the future prosperity and health of a family and were usually well paid for their services. This obviously made the profession an attractive option for charlatans. Thus it is easy to see why so many western observers of *feng shui* considered it an entirely false science and poured scorn on its practice and practitioners.

The scholar Joseph Needham is not so dismissive of *feng shui* in his work on *Science and Civilisation in China*:

> In many ways *feng shui* was an advantage to the Chinese people, as when, for example, it advised planting trees and bamboos as windbreaks, and emphasized the value of flowing water adjacent to a house site. In other ways it developed into a grossly superstitious system. But all through, it embodied, I believe, a marked aesthetic component, which accounts for the great beauty of siting of so many farms, houses and villages throughout China.

Communities often clubbed together to pay for a pagoda to be built on a hillside to improve the *feng shui* of a locality. The pagoda would sometimes have no religious significance whatsoever, but always had the merit of being an attractive feature in the landscape. One can only wish that the aesthetic aspects of *feng shui* were still respected in contemporary building programmes in China.

Influence on Design

The importance of *feng shui* in the architecture of China is nowhere more apparent than in the siting of imperial tombs. The traditional geomancy of tomb siting favoured a setting of winding tracks, curving rivers and undulating hills, thus imperial tomb sites are never approached in a straight line and are usually 'protected' by high ground at the rear and at the front a curved watercourse, (natural by preference, but artificial if necessary), crossed by a set of arched bridges. Once inside the tomb compound, however, there was a return to the strict axiality which was typical of palace architecture, and the halls and courtyards of the ancestral spirits echoed the shapes and structures of the mansions of the living. The tomb itself was constructed underground which in Ming and Qing times had coffin chambers of long, brick, arched vaults. The underground vaults were usually covered by a circular earth mound and surrounded by a circular wall (the circle as the symbol of Heaven was deemed appropriate for the last resting place of the corpse). The tomb had also to be well-drained so that no water accumulated on the tomb site, because this was inauspicious (and in the practical sense undesirable as it would accelerate the decay of the corpse and the sacrificial offerings buried within the coffin). Drainage channels in imperial tombs were often extensive and elaborate.

As well as tombs, official and sacrificial buildings were also influenced by cosmology and geomancy. Although cosmology tended to influence the forms of buildings for the living, and geomancy the siting of tombs, the two systems of ideas were often used together. They were also sometimes used as a pretext for a political manoeuvre, (one Ming dynasty Minister of the Board of Rites, in the Wan Li reign, was dismissed on the spurious grounds that he had not selected an auspicious enough site for the emperor's tomb), and even used by an emperor as an excuse to do or not do something for personal reasons. An emperor could always find an ambiguity of text or argument to cast aside the requests of his officials if he so desired, and court officials could always use precedence or portents to force an emperor into or out of a scheme. In short, it is important to remember that the Chinese people have always been as pragmatic as they have been superstitious and that court ritual and religion could be as significant or as meaningless as the emperor and his court so desired. And in looking at 'imperial' China, one also has to bear in mind that the intellectual world of the second-century BC Han emperors was a very different place from the realities of late Qing dynasty emperors, who had to deal with the arrival on their shores of western soldiers, science, merchants and missionaries. In the two thousand years between the first and last emperors of China, elements of court ritual and religion had remained constant, but the world had not.

The Imperial System

The Chinese empire should not be viewed as an immutable monolith which, after two thousand years, suddenly toppled and fell in the 20th century. Unwieldy, fragile and unattractive as it must have seemed to most observers in 1911, at its demise, the Chinese empire had had long periods of strength and stability, despite eras of decline, war and fragmentation. For two thousand years, with interruptions, it had proved to be the world's best organized, flexible and stable political institution, feeding and controlling a complex and populous agrarian society. Its best emperors were men of extraordinary talent, intelligence and vigour; its worst were lazy fools, prisoners of their own palaces, beset by factionalism and intrigue which they were unable or unwilling to control. It was generally the case that the early emperors of a dynasty moulded the system to their liking, which in turn moulded and made puppets of the later emperors.

The Scholar as Administrator

The most remarkable feature of the Chinese imperial system was not so much the semi-divine role of the emperor, a feature of many civilizations, but rather the rule of the scholar-bureaucrat. Educated in moral philosophy, history and state-craft, based on a set of Confucian classical texts, and recruited by a complex and demanding examination system, he was expected to undertake any type of work without specialist training. This system produced a great degree of orthodoxy of thought and, in times of stability under a strong emperor, a well-run and conscientious civil service. Even under a weak emperor, the civil service could function reasonably efficiently in carrying out established routines. However, an indecisive ruler caused factionalism in the upper echelons of the civil service, which usually prevented any major, and sometimes vital, decisions being made.

(Below and Opposite) A statue of a civlian high official in the Spirit Avenue of the Ming Tombs.

Civil servants were recruited from all walks of life, and successful exam candidates were often the sons of peasants, educated by a village, clan or government organization. Only the sons of actors, butchers and prostitutes were denied this career. Such a meritocratic civil service gave society a ruling class which retained wealth and position only through the continued success of sons in the imperial exam. Since official rank was the only path to social eminence, a great family which failed to produce successful scholars was soon doomed to oblivion. A strong merchant class did develop, which managed to create and maintain large family fortunes outside of this system, but because the social prestige of the businessman was low, merchants often invested heavily in the education of their sons.

The Confucian education, on which the syllabus of the imperial examination was based, involved the study of the Four Classics, documents from the Zhou dynasty believed to have been collated by Confucius (551–479 BC). These had the near status of holy writ. The Four Classics are the *Shi Jing*, the 'Book of Songs', which is an anthology of ancient poetry; the *Shu Jing*, the 'Classic of Documents', an historical work; the *Yi Jing*, the 'Book of Changes', a manual for divination; and the *Li Ji*, the 'Record of Rites', a text on ritual and ceremony. These Four Classics were the cornerstone of a Confucian education and inculcated a sense of history, moral outlook, ceremonial behaviour and a gentlemanly code of conduct in those who studied them.

The Philosophy of State Confucianism

Although Confucianism was the basis of a scholar's education for the imperial examination, it was not the only school of philosophy to shape statecraft. During the late Zhou era, after the collapse of the central authority of the Zhou kings — a time known as the **Warring States Period** (475–221 BC) — many philosophers, including Confucius, taught at the courts of the feudal princes. Their job was to devise strategies for the maintenance of good government, and, in some cases, strategies for winning wars. The philosophers, who came to be known collectively as 'Confucians', held the central tenet that moral authority and the welfare of the people should be the ruler's central considerations. The 'Mandate of Heaven' was a central tenet of Confucianism because Confucius looked to the early years of the Zhou dynasty as a golden age and the founding rulers as sage emperors. Other philosophers, termed Legalists, argued that a highly structured state with laws and harsh penal code was the solution. Yet other philosophers, of the Daoist school, expounded a form of poetic iconoclasm advising the wise scholar to retreat from office and worldly affairs and achieve 'oneness' with the natural world. The ideal Daoist ruler was portrayed as one who achieves harmony of

13

government by transcendental non-action or *wu wei*. In the Han dynasty, when the philosophical basis of the imperial system was largely evolved, ideas from all three philosophical traditions were woven together, with Confucianism as the dominant element.

In state Confucianism, the most important philosopher, second only to Confucius, was Mencius (c. 372–289 BC). A follower of Confucian thought, Mencius argued for a moral and just society ruled by virtue rather than by law. In many ways, his philosophy was revolutionary: he wrote that in the state 'the people are of most importance; the spirits of the land and grain are next; and the sovereign is insignificant'. He advocated 'civil' rather than 'military' virtues in a ruler. The founding emperor of the Ming dynasty, **Hong Wu**, (reigned 1368–98), whose title means 'Grand Warrior', was very proud of his military prowess. He disliked Mencian concepts so intensely that he had them deleted from the national syllabus in 1367 when he restored the civil service examinations. However, his grandson, and his successor, the **Jian Wen** emperor (reigned 1399–1402), whose title aptly means 'Establish the Civil', overturned the edict on Mencius. Thereafter, Mencius remained in the Ming and Qing civil service syllabus, despite the militaristic tendencies of many emperors.

The syllabus of state Confucianism created a largely orthodox and enlightened group of scholars whom the emperor could call upon to act as administrators. But state orthodoxy was not without its inner conflicts. The idea of the ruler reigning through virtue contrasted sharply with his very real responsibilities to consolidate his power, enrich the state and maintain an effective army.

Rule by divine inertia also did not tally with the demands of Confucian statecraft, with its endless round of rites, ceremonies and consultations with ministers. Yet, somehow, all three heterodox strands did combine in imperial statecraft, to a greater or lesser degree of success depending on the character and inclinations of each individual emperor. Most strong rulers did go to war as part of their policy to extend Chinese control over the distant border regions; most also patronized the arts and scholarship, took part in state rituals and commissioned state architecture. The able emperors understood the need to balance political necessity with visibly virtuous conduct. However, some sovereigns did exceptionally well in the category of non-action: the Ming dynasty Wan Li emperor became so disaffected with his bureaucracy that he refused to grant an audience or sign a document for 25 years. Sadly, such a tactic was of no benefit to him or his dynasty: within 24 years of his death in 1620, the Ming house was to perish.

The Emperor and the Civil Service

Emperors were wise to treat their civil service with respect. It was, after all, the eyes and hands of the ruler, and he could not act without it. When used effectively, the civil service could coordinate enormous tasks such as irrigation works and flood control, which, if left in the hands of local interests, could founder for lack of central planning. It could also initiate major building programmes such as the Great Wall. If the civil service was demoralized, effective government at the local level and the all-important task of tax-collection could break down, thus jeopardizing the very existence of the state.

Regulating the civil service was a fine balancing act. Should an emperor be over-zealous in his jurisdiction of his servants, he could risk passive resistance from those unhappy with their tasks. Should he neglect his civil service and fail to control and balance the power groups within the bureaucracy, then factionalism and the inevitable policy zig-zags or drift could undermine and even destroy his power to act effectively in crisis. The last Ming emperors ensured the downfall of their house in the face of insurrection and the threat of the Manchus from the north simply because factionalism had left them helpless and suspicious in their dealings with ministers. This meant that no one policy could be pursued effectively for very long, because no minister was in a secure enough position to guarantee that his decisions would be carried out.

As a ruler of divine significance, the emperor commanded loyalty and obedience of a great magnitude, but it was his position rather than his person that made him the Son of Heaven. Senior civil servants who had daily contact with an incompetent sovereign suffered no illusions about their ruler's failings. Although this did not usually undermine their loyalty to the throne, it could often lead to an endless flow of critical memorials admonishing the emperor and reminding him of his duties. For enshrined within the imperial system was the right of an official to memorialize the throne. And because these memorials were always recorded by the court historians for posterity, it meant that the emperor risked his reputation in the dynastic histories if he did not deal wisely. This procedure often restrained emperors from rash or unworthy action, but sometimes it led to the public flogging or death of the official who had angered his sovereign with moral rebukes. Yet even such extreme reactions failed to deter the more principled government servants from sending memorials. They felt that the honour and burden of their position demanded outspokenness, and even death, if necessary. Death only meant that their integrity would be recorded for posterity, and an honourable name often meant more than life.

The Role of the Eunuchs

Whereas able emperors could harness the energy and idealism of their civil servants to undertake weighty tasks of administration, incompetent emperors, usually because they distrusted their officials and feared their criticisms, often turned to court eunuchs to carry out their bidding. A feature of palace life from the earliest of dynasties, eunuchs could create a major problem in the balance of power at court. Their official function was to act as household servants and guards in the imperial precincts, but in reality they could become important power-brokers because they had direct access to the emperor and may have been part of his household for many years.

Emperors brought up entirely within the palace walls, such as those of the later Ming dynasty, were surrounded from birth by eunuchs who often became trusted friends and confidants. Many emperors, such as the **Jia Jing** (reigned 1522–66) and **Tian Qi** (reigned 1621–27) emperors of the Ming era, let eunuchs take over decision-making in the administration of the empire, while they retreated into hobbies, leisure or pleasure. The Jia Jing emperor was a dabbler in alchemy and an active patron of building projects around the capital (all but one of the suburban altars in Peking date from his reign). The Tian Qi emperor found the affairs of state too wearisome and took up carpentry.

The Jia Jing emperor of the Ming dynasty.

Even able and powerful emperors such as the Ming **Yong Le** emperor (the architectural patron of imperial Peking, who reigned 1402–24) used eunuchs as trusted servants and spies, despite the edict from his father, the first Ming emperor, that eunuchs were to be used only for household duties and were banned from undertaking official functions. In 1420, Yong Le set up an institution known as the Eastern Depot and, under its auspices, used eunuchs for surveillance operations. Under later emperors, the Eastern Depot became famous as a torture chamber for officials who had provoked imperial anger.

The Qing Bureaucracy

The Qing emperors, like their Ming predecessors, also used eunuchs as state employees. They were allowed to undertake such lucrative tasks as tax collection and supervision of imperial tomb construction — always an opportunity for embezzlement on a grand scale. Qing government structure was further complicated by a layer of Manchu officials at every level to counterbalance the number of native Chinese civil servants. This doubling of government servants aimed at ensuring that the foreign ruling house had its own people on the ground as well as creating employment for its loyal followers. This system was much resented by Chinese officials and created an additional burden for the treasury. Such a burden was not too onerous in the reigns of fiscally astute monarchs such as Kang Xi and **Yong Zheng** (reigned 1723–35). However, later emperors, who were less able and also faced the problems of a growing population, an antiquated tax collection system and the threat of foreign invasion, could not adequately control official expenditure and the downfall of the empire was thereby hastened.

Chinese Architecture — Principles and Evolution

In the long history of Chinese civilization, the written records compiled by court officials give few details of the history of architecture. It was not an admired scholar's art as calligraphy, painting and poetry were. A well-constructed and well-sited building, like a fine piece of porcelain, would have been appreciated and commissioned by emperor or scholar, but it would have been designed by a master-craftsman. The names of a few educated and talented architects have been recorded, but most master-builders would have been, at best, semi-literate, and their skills would have been transmitted orally to their sons or apprentices. Architects who worked as respected and highly paid individuals with the social status of a European court composer or painter, were not a feature of traditional Chinese society.

However, senior court officials often took responsibility for the supervision of the construction of palaces and tombs. They had to make sure that the site was well chosen by the geomancers and that there was no misappropriation of funds (ironically many of those officials, frequently eunuchs, took their assignment as a golden opportunity to become embezzlers-in-chief!). However, one scholar bureaucrat, Li Jie of the **Song dynasty** (960–1279), took such an educated interest in his supervisory work that he learned the skills of a practising builder and in 1100 compiled a manual, the *Ying Zao Fa Shi* or 'Treatise on Architectural Methods' with detailed illustrations of contemporary architectural technology and design. This has been an excellent source book for architectural historians, who have had so few buildings of that period to study. Manuals of the later Ming and Qing periods have survived, too, which illustrate the kinds of buildings that we can still see today. Thus, Chinese architecture has not been shaped by the works of individual creative geniuses, but rather by the craftsman, his copy-book and well-worn rules.

Yet those rules have not been immutable. Change has come from interpretation and reinterpretation. Also, the destruction of successive dynasties, the move of capitals, the invasions of nomadic peoples, the hiring of craftsmen from other lands and the introduction of Buddhism all affected architectural styles, evidence of which can still be seen today. From the differences between the illustrations in architectural manuals from the Song and later dynasties, we know that the dynamics of construction of imperial architecture have undergone radical transformations from the setting of the pitch of the roof to the solution of weight distribution on columns. We also know from these manuals that the base unit of measure for building, which set the ratio for length, width and height and allowed widespread standardization in Chinese architecture, was gauged differently in the Song and later Ming and Qing dynastic periods.

Interestingly, in contrast with Western architecture, building materials and patterns for groundplans for traditional architecture changed little since earliest times. Even the thatched roof was preserved by scholars eager to create a pastoral retreat. The custom of placing all major buildings on a platform of compacted earth or stone, essentially to protect them against damp, is as ancient as the thatch, but, unlike the thatch, the platform remained in common usage up until the middle of this century. All important halls and pavilions were raised above ground level in Chinese architecture.

Building Materials

The fretwork of wooden columns and beams that is the skeleton of all traditional Chinese houses is believed to date back to the earliest times. Only in defensive works were load-bearing walls built (and those walls frequently featured arches, an element conspicuously absent from residential architecture). However, where a building was needed for storage or the safe-keeping of valuables, such as the Imperial Archives, walls were built of brick and stone in order to minimize the risk of fire.

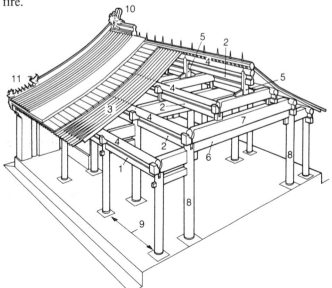

Diagram to show structural composition of a Chinese hall with gable roof
1. Architrave;
2. Longitudinal tie-beam;
3. Rafters;
4. Purlin;
5. Strut;
6. Transversal tie-beam;
7. Beam;
8. Column;
9. Bay;
10. Acroterion;
11. Roof guardians.

In most residential architecture, all the weight of the roof was carried on the wooden columns, not the walls. In the earliest buildings the walls were made of wattle and daub or baked mud; later they were plaster partitions between the pillars. Because the columns carried the weight of the roof, the builder had great freedom in placing walls, door and windows, which explains why so many monumental buildings have the lightest walls of delicate lattice. In the south of China, where builders had to allow good ventilation during the intensely hot summers, south-facing façades were often left open to the air or were given lattice-work frames. In contrast, northern buildings had to be insulated against cold in winter and well-ventilated in summer, so shutter doors were fitted which could be folded open in hot weather. Where wood was a scarce commodity, and this has been the case in most of north China for the past few centuries, ordinary people had to make their homes with bricks, or, in the loess lands of the north-west, excavate hillsides to make cave dwellings. Such cave houses are still a common sight in the countryside around such a city as Xi'an in China's north-west Shanxi province. But for the emperors, with vast funds at their disposal, the purchase of timber was rarely any problem.

The earliest roofs would have been made of natural materials such as straw, reeds or branches mixed with mud, yet as early as by the eighth century BC, clay tiles are believed to have been in common usage for major buildings. These tiles were made in semi-circular profile, and were much larger than the ones we see today in traditional architecture. Such early tiles that have survived show relief patterns, a feature of tile-making that remained a distinctive element in Chinese roof design until the early years of this century.

Relief design of an animal on a Han dynasty tile end.

Our first chance to see what early Chinese buildings must have looked like comes from carved reliefs and model buildings found in Han burial chambers of the second century BC, which tell us much about an era from which no building has survived. It seems that the distinctive curved roof of Chinese buildings had not yet evolved in this period. All roof outlines depicted in the tombs are straight, although one or two examples display upturned eaves. But it is evident that the technique of placing tiles in alternate and overlapping convex and concave lines dates back to at least this era.

Lacquer has also been another important material in the history of Chinese building. Its use dates back to the Shang period and then, as now, it was used for preserving and decorating wood. Lacquer is derived from the sap of the lacquer tree, *Rhus vernicifera*, and when applied in a series of thin layers, forms a surface that is resistant to acid as well as water. Its decorative qualities were also appreciated from the earliest of times. Mixed with cinnabar, lacquer could be coloured red; with iron sulphate, a lustrous black could be achieved. Bronze-age pre-imperial texts tell of the importance of colour in denoting rank when building: red pillars were reserved for the palace of the ruler, black for the princes and blue-green for the nobles. Red remained the colour for the ruler all through Chinese imperial history. In later centuries, lacquer was also carved and inlaid with precious metals.

A clay model of an early Chinese building excavated from a Han dynasty tomb. Of interest are the two storeys and straight roof lines.

Paint was and has remained an important element in decorating buildings. Because Chinese buildings traditionally had an open framework where the interior beams and rafters were left exposed to the eye, there was much scope for painted decoration on the internal and external woodwork of the buildings. Paint, like lacquer, also helped to preserve the timber. The earliest painted designs were from mythology and nature: dragons (a constant motif in the decoration of buildings for rulers), horses (popular in the Han and Tang periods of increased contact with Central Asia), trees and plants. By late imperial times, two major styles of painting on timber had evolved: the official palace style known as *he xi*, and the pleasure garden style known as *Su shi* or the Suzhou style (Suzhou is a city in central eastern China famous for its small landscaped gardens.) The *he xi* style was used for decorating all the official and ceremonial buildings of the emperor, and featured central panels of gilded dragons and phoenixes and a pattern known as the 'whirling flower' design. The whirling flower is a versatile and variable design which was used with great ingenuity in the intermediate panels between the dragon and phoenix motifs. The dominant colours of the *he xi* style are gold, blue and green. In contrast, the *Su shi* style of painting featured central panels of landscapes and scenes with birds, animals and flowers. It often featured *trompe l'oeil* effects, which were introduced into Chinese art by Jesuit painters at the Chinese court in the 17th and 18th centuries.

Whirling flower pattern in the *he xi* style of decoration.

文思光被

A detail of interior painted panels of the Long Gallery in the Garden of Ease and Harmony illustrating the *Su shi* or Suzhou-style of decoration.

In the grandest halls, gold leaf would also have been used for decoration. The inside of the main throne hall of the Forbidden City, the Hall of Supreme Harmony has six central pillars featuring relief carvings of spiralling dragons which are covered in gold leaf and applied in two contrasting tones. It is likely that such gilded pillars were a feature of the lost palaces of earlier dynasties.

Layout and Composition

In their use of materials Chinese builders clearly did not build for posterity. This is in marked contrast to the great stone cathedrals of Europe, which bear testimony to the enduring art of medieval stonemasons. The tall, vaulted cathedrals also underline another fundamental difference between western and Chinese architecture: the use of space on the horizontal and vertical planes. Chinese buildings, even the very grandest, rarely reach beyond two storeys in height. Expansion in the Chinese plan is made on the horizontal plane with the multiplication of courtyards and buildings around the main axis. The multi-storeyed pagoda or stupa is the exception to this rule, but scholars agree that its origins were Indian rather than Chinese. Look-out towers and multi-storey dwellings were known to have been built in the Han dynasty, but this tradition does not adequately presage the five-, seven-, and up to thirteen-storeyed pagodas that are now so much a part of the landscape of China. It was the spread of Buddhism to China from India in the late Han period and the following centuries that was to make the pagoda a common feature of Chinese architecture, not only within the compound of a Buddhist monastery but also on the hillsides and by the waterways of the Chinese countryside.

A clay model of a three-storey tower excavated from a Han dynasty tomb.

A comparison of the approach to a European cathedral with a Chinese palace or temple hall yields yet another interesting insight. Medieval cathedrals were designed to be approached from the transversal or western end, and it was here that the medieval craftsmen created wonderful exterior carvings which were the showpiece of external decoration. The cathedrals were constructed to impress with height from the exterior (think of the twin towers of Chartres cathedral or the two rising ladders on the west face of Bath Abbey), and depth when viewed from the interior (picture the soaring vaults of Amiens or Rheims cathedrals). But Chinese palace halls were designed to be approached from the south side or on the long axis. Balance and harmony of aspect were the desired effect. The Chinese building was measured in 'bays' (*jian*), or the spaces between columns, thus the grander a building, the larger the number of bays and columns set out on the longitudinal side. The transverse side of the building was not designed to be viewed and would feature very little decoration except for a gold ribbon and ball design on the gable ends of important imperial buildings. This does not mean that Chinese buildings are not imposing, it is just that they achieve that effect through different means.

From as early as the Zhou dynasty, we know that Chinese cities were oriented on a north–south axis. Cities were laid out to create a series of enclosed squares and rectangles set behind defensive walls. Gates were usually placed in the walls on the four cardinal points — north, south, east and west. North gates were sometimes not built because, in Chinese tradition, the north is the direction from which baleful influences or spirits approach human habitation, and thus their passage must be blocked.

This blocking off of the northern wall was as much a feature of private residential compounds as cities. Traditionally, no Chinese house had its main entrance on the north side; south was the favoured direction. The Forbidden City in Peking does have a northern gate, the Gate of Martial Spirit, but the rear of the city is protected by the hill known as Prospect Hill (or Coal Hill). Of cosmic significance, the Forbidden City was built to reflect and enhance the harmony of the heavens. Its ground-plan of a sequence of halls, courtyards and gates running in a continuous line on a north–south axis creates a series of architectural climaxes not seen in any building complex elsewhere in the world.

The north–south axis may dominate Chinese architectural planning, but it is by no means ubiquitous. Where topography demanded, the axis could be shifted to take in the benefits of scenic views or features such as waterways or hills. Pleasure palaces were planned with little heed to the cardinal points and with much attention to scenic advantage.

The north–south axis was strictly adhered to in buildings with a cosmological significance, such as the Temple of Heaven where, in the Ming and Qing periods, the emperor made sacrifices to Heaven at the winter solstice. However, in the imperial tombs, strict axiality gave way to accommodate the need for good *feng shui*. The tombs and their Spirit Avenues, through which the coffin approached its final resting place, would usually be sited on the slopes of south-facing hills and the important elements in their layout would be the felicitous combinations of 'breaths' or 'cosmic currents' (known as *qi*) which were believed to move through the hillsides and watercourses.

The Chinese predilection for symmetrical, gridiron, north–south-oriented city plans is mirrored in microcosm in the planning of the family home. Courtyards would be approached from the south and the main hall would be set on the north side of the courtyard, facing south. The east and west sides of the courtyard would have buildings of lesser impor-

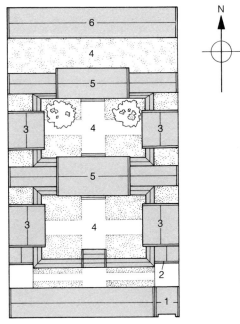

N

Plan of a typical traditional courtyard dwelling
1. Street entrance;
2. Screen wall;
3. Side halls (residential quarters);
4. Open courtyard;
5. Main halls;
6. Rear halls (residential quarters of head of household).

tance. The richer the household, the more courtyards there would be, with family groups allocated their own halls or whole courtyards. Many of these traditional one-storey courtyard complexes, known as *si he yuan*, have survived to this day in Peking. If you climb the Drum Tower, to the north of the Forbidden City, you can see below a sea of small dusty grey roofs arranged in courtyards. The plan of the courtyard is less easy to see these days because the pressure on living space has meant that many courtyard gardens have been built over and little open space has been left. But, occasionally, it is possible to glimpse an open courtyard with trees (undoubtedly the residence of a high-ranking Communist Party official), and enjoy the humanity of scale of the traditional courtyard dwelling.

The private living quarters of the Forbidden City echo this pattern of residential building with a maze of small courtyards, halls and gardens spread out to the north of the central section of imposing ceremonial halls, vast open courtyards and monumental gates. But in terms of space, the emperor's private living quarters were little grander than those of his relatives and officials.

The homes of rich and noble families were also as enclosed as the living quarters of the emperor, if not as well guarded. For, unlike European grand houses or palaces, which were built to be seen, Chinese homes or imperial residences were traditionally enclosed behind high, blank walls. Passers-by could not even catch a glimpse of the buildings within the walls because the gate, if left open, would have its entrance space screened by a free-standing wall. These walls have come to be known in the west as 'spirit walls' or 'screens', because of the Chinese belief that ghosts can travel in straight lines only, and so cannot turn a corner to enter a household if the gateway is blocked by a screen wall. However, it is quite apparent that the main practical function of these walls was to provide privacy for members of the household. Chinese builders therefore had no reason to create diverse and original façades for family mansions.

The façades were never meant to be seen as symbols of prestige or wealth, and were, as a consequence, built in a standard fashion with the level of decoration suitable to the rank of the occupants. Only the colour of the tiles on the roof would tell outsiders the status of those who dwelt within. Yellow was the imperial colour and only the emperor's residences could have yellow-tiled roofs, but princes and the highest officials could use glazed green tiles for their roofs. Ordinary city folk had to be content with unglazed grey tiles. Buildings were thus set out and decorated with a strong sense of status and tradition.

Civil service rank would determine how many bays and columns an official was allowed to build. No Chinese courtier would ever have dared to create the equivalent of the Duke of Marlborough's Blenheim Palace or a Loire château. Private wealth in China would have been put into fine art collections and the creation of gardens rather than the building of palatial mansions to rival those of the emperor. And anyway, the building of too grand a mansion or tomb could, if the news of it reached the ears of the emperor, cost the life of the presumptuous official.

Traditional Chinese buildings have a structural composition which falls into three distinct layers: the roof; the support pillars and enclosing walls; and the raised foundations. The most important element in the composition was always the roof, and it was here that Chinese craftsmen excelled themselves in ingenuity and versatility of design in comparison with their western counterparts. The supporting pillars, sometimes left open to create a peristyle or open gallery, sometimes enclosed by a wall, played an important, but less emphatic part in the balance of the composition. It was only where the pillars met the tie-beams underneath the eaves that the artistry of the craftsmen was given full rein. The raised foundations would be designed to balance and complement the weight and span of the roof.

Roof Construction

The pronounced concave curve of the roof is perhaps the first feature that strikes the eye when looking at a Chinese building. Such a roof looks more picturesque, and somehow less functional, than the straight roofs of the West. Yet, as exotic as they may look, curved roofs with overhanging eaves have many practical advantages: they allow efficient water run-off, well away from the walls of the building; they are stable in high winds (an important feature in the blustery days of a north China spring); they provide protection from the harsh glare of

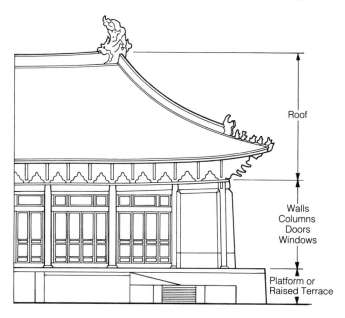

Three layers of composition in a traditional Chinese wooden building.

Roof

Walls
Columns
Doors
Windows

Platform or
Raised Terrace

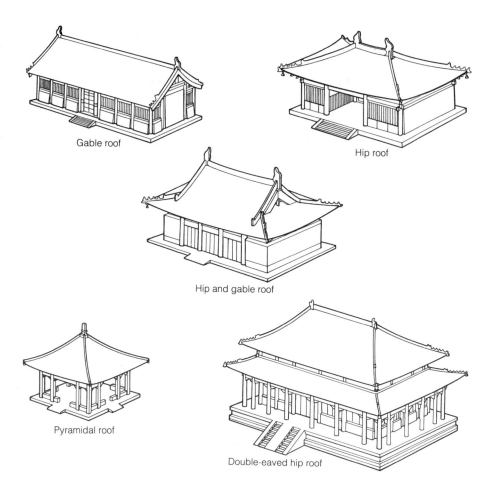

Gable roof

Hip roof

Hip and gable roof

Pyramidal roof

Double-eaved hip roof

Four basic roof types, and an example of a double-eaved roof.

the summer sun while also allowing the low-angled rays of the winter sun to penetrate to the interior. However, as practical in their function as they were, these roofs were mainly built for aesthetic effect.

In most traditional buildings, the builder would plan his work on the basis of how many bays were needed. The roof would then be designed to match the required length and depth of the building. There were four distinct roof types (not allowing for regional variation and special roofs designed for specific purposes) he could choose from: hip; hip and gable; gable; and pyramidal. All these roof types could be built with one or more layers. Traditionally, the most important palace buildings had a hip roof, usually with double eaves, lesser palace roofs were built in the hip-and-gable style, and ordinary homes were most likely to be built with gable roofs. The builder could also put up polygonal, circular or Greek cross-shaped roofs of one or more layers to greater decorative effect. Such roofs were most commonly reserved for the pavilions of garden or palace architecture. Temple halls, which had to house a large Buddha image, had roofs of special and distinctive design. In palace construction, the balancing of sequences of buildings with different roof shapes and heights was a fine art.

In theory, the Chinese architect had great freedom to set the pitch and curve of his roof. In reality, however, precedents in building practice did lead to conscious constraint, particularly in imperial architecture. The reason for the freedom to set the curve of the roof was the absence of the rigid triangular truss. The western tradition of roof building has been less playful and imaginative than that of China because the preferred method of roof construction with a rigid truss does not allow any change of angle in the laying of the rafters.

The early Chinese knew of the triangular truss form, but preferred to build their roofs above a structure of rising rectangular layers that rested on columns of equal height. (There was a tradition of building with columns of rising height, but the equal-height column structure has always been more widespread.) These rectangular layers would diminish in

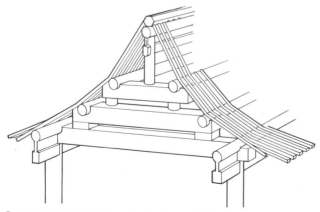

Stepped truss roof structure showing layers of rafters

29

A roof built in the southern Chinese style with high, upswinging eaves and elaborate roof decoration, Yu Garden, Shanghai.

size towards the top. The gradation of height and size of these layers one above the other allowed the builder to pitch the roof as he liked. In the architecture of south China, a tradition evolved of building roofs with deep curves, extravagant upswinging eaves and, in many cases, a curved concave roof ridge. On the other hand, the northern architectural tradition, which encompasses most imperial architecture, shows more restrained roof construction. There are also distinct regional variations in roof colours and decoration, with bright primary colours popular in the north, black, greys and white common in central eastern China (look at the garden architecture of Suzhou in Jiangsu province), and highly elaborate and coloured roof sculptures in the southern provinces (Canton city temples are some of the most memorable).

From a comparison of buildings of different dates and illustrations from architectural manuals, we can see that the pitch of the roof has not always been determined by the same methods. During the Song dynasty, craftsmen set the first layer below the roof ridge at a distance of one-tenth the measure of the vertical line between the roof ridge and the eaves. The second level was set at one twentieth, and the third at one-fortieth. This gave the roofs a great elasticity of curve and, as a consequence, much beauty of form. Sadly, few buildings of the Song era have survived; one of the best preserved is in the city of Taiyuan in Shanxi province: the Shengmu Hall of the Jinci Temple. The structure is a double-eaved hip roof seven bays wide, with the broad gently tapering roof line and heavy column brackets of the classical Song style. Unfortunately, no comparable building exists in Peking.

Builders of the later Ming and Qing dynasties set their roofs on an upward-moving calculation with a pitch of greater rigidity and straightness of line. In this later period, the emphasis was on elegance of line and a decorative effect rather than structural innovation. Most art historians feel that the later roofs, the best illustrations of which can be seen in northern imperial architecture, are less inventive and dramatic than their Song precursors. Only in the garden architecture of the Ming period, found in central-eastern China, do you find echoes of that exuberance and dynamism which was the hallmark of the earlier builders. In order to have an idea of how the roofs of buildings of the Tang dynasty must have looked, you have to go to the Buddhist temples of Japan, many of which were recreations of buildings Japanese pilgrims saw on their journeys through Tang China.

Because most Chinese traditional buildings were 'open-frame', and the exposed structure was made part of the visual design, it is possible to look up inside a building and see how the roof was put together. The traditional craftsman needed no metal nails in his joinery; most of the timber pieces were assembled in complex interlocking joints in order to give flexibility and stability. These joints, or tenons and mortices, were of different design depending on the angle, weight and position of the timbers. The Song manual *Ying Zao Fa Shi* contains good illustrations of types of tenons and mortices.

Metal nails were needed only in the setting of the rafters. These were not laid in one continuous straight line, as they are in western roofs, but were layered in short strips in order to allow the curve of the roof to be formed. A convex roof ridge could be achieved by placing two upright timbers, or queen-posts, of equal height either side of the central ridge-line. Tiles were held in place by wooden pins on the ridge-line and by lime on the slopes.

The Bracket Set

However, it was in the method of distributing the weight of the roof on the supporting columns that Chinese craftsmen achieved their greatest masterpieces of integration of design and function — by means of the bracket set, or *dou gong*. We know from archaeological evidence that bracket sets were developed as early as the Han dynasty, for we can see them reproduced in stone on Han funerary columns found in Sichuan province, and in clay on the model houses placed in many of the tombs of this period. The bracket set was a rising

Diagram to show a
column set of the
Song dynasty
1. Flying rafters;
2. Eave rafters;
3. Eave purlin;
4. Ang;
5. Beak of the ang;
6. Beam;
7. Lintel or architrave.

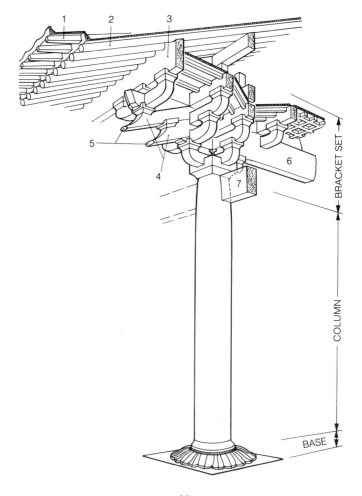

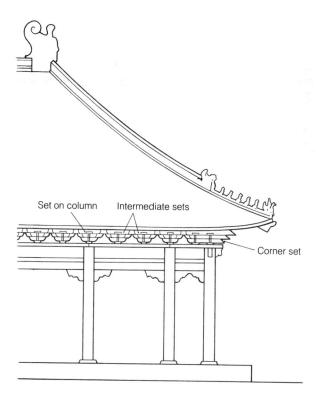

Diagram to show positions of bracket sets.

Set on column

Intermediate sets

Corner set

tier of interlocking arms and brackets which allowed the heavy weight of the roof to be distributed on the supporting columns of the building. They were of prime importance as walls in Chinese buildings were rarely load-bearing and thus played no part in holding up the weight of the roof. With the addition of the bracket set, columns could hold a weight calculated to be about five times greater than that which could be supported without such a bracket. Bracket sets were placed either directly on the column or along the architraves between the columns. Those above the columns are known as 'column sets'; those between the columns are called 'intermediate sets'.

Song dynasty builders were extremely inventive in their use of the bracket set and also added angled cantilever arms, or *ang*, to help with the distribution of weight. The bracket sets of this period were built to great dramatic effect and were very large in relation to the height of their supporting columns — they could be of a size of one-third to half the height of their

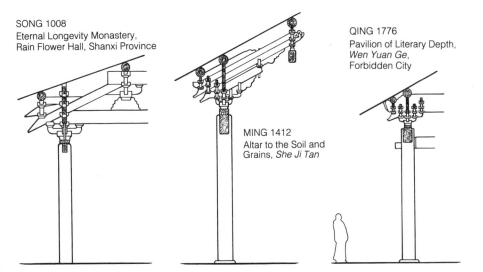

SONG 1008
Eternal Longevity Monastery,
Rain Flower Hall, Shanxi Province

QING 1776
Pavilion of Literary Depth,
Wen Yuan Ge,
Forbidden City

MING 1412
Altar to the Soil and
Grains, *She Ji Tan*

Evolution of the bracket set or Chinese 'order'.

supporting columns. By the time of the Ming dynasty, bracket sets had shrunk in size and had become one-fifth or less of the height of the column. Their load-bearing function by this time was vestigial: column sets still had a structural role but the intermediate sets served only a decorative function. As a result, the tie-beams of the Ming period and later were larger than their precursors and were designed more as girders.

The number of bracket sets used along the line of the eaves also increased in the Ming and Qing periods. In most of the imperial buildings we see in China today, these bracket sets have an almost entirely decorative function, with the Song *ang*, or cantilever arm, only echoed as a non-functional design element, projecting at an angle from the bracket set like a blunt-ended bird's beak. Because Ming and Qing architecture is so distinctive in having more intermediate bracket sets than earlier architecture, it is usually quite easy to determine how old a building is by counting the number of bracket sets between the columns. Five or more will tell you that the building is likely to be of the Ming period or later. (Nevertheless it is important to remember that many old buildings in China have been renovated many times since they were first built and that later features can sometimes be found grafted onto earlier buildings.)

Roof Decoration

Roof decoration, as well as design, has always been a key element in the overall composition. The brilliantly coloured expanses of roof tiles set in undulating rows are designed to bring the eye up to see the lines and mass of the roof. Early pictures and models of roofs show that there is an ancient tradition of decorating the ends of the ridge and the eaves with small figures and beasts; these were to ward off evil spirits, protect the buildings from fire and express the power and authority of the occupant. The more important the building, the greater the number of roof figurines there were lined up above the corner edges of the eaves.

The acroteria, *chi wen*, or roof ridge-end sculptures, of later buildings in imperial compounds feature open-mouthed drag-

Eave-end roof guardians, the Forbidden City.

ons seemingly swallowing the roof ridge. But we do know that the earlier acroteria from the pre-Ming period featured designs of upsweeping fish tails, believed to be a magic symbol that protected the building from fire. The dragon acroteria of the Drum and Bell Tower in Peking are outward-facing horned dragons that ward off the evil spirits which fly through the air. All these roof sculptures and figures add to the dominance of the roof in the structural composition of the building.

Further colour was applied to the eaves, bracket sets and the interior of the roof with painted designs. As most of the timber framework of the interior of the roof was visible, paint played an important dual function of decoration and preservation. Set out on the beams would be painted panels: dragon and phoenix motifs in the halls of court, and ornamental scenes in the pavilions and halls of the pleasure parks.

Acroterion in the shape of an open-mouthed dragon. Acroteria on more important ceremonial buildings are larger and, in addition, have a decorative dagger set in their back with a handle shaped like three fronds.

35

Ceilings, as such, were not common features of traditional Chinese buildings. However, some important staterooms did have flat coffered ceilings put in, with a recurring pattern painted on every ceiling panel. In the most important throne halls, where solemn ceremonies were held, you can see 'lantern ceilings' — a clever design of rising layers of timbers that create circles within squares within octagons. All these shapes had important cosmic meanings: the circle represented heaven; the square symbolized earth and the octagon was the shape of the ancient divination system known as the *Yi Jing* or *I Ching*, where there are eight symbolic sets of three broken and unbroken lines set around an octagon. It was beneath such ceilings that the emperor was believed to commune with heaven in prayer before sacrifices or visits to the ancestral temple.

Walls and Pillars

In the central section of the structure of a traditional building, the pillars and walls created a contrast of restraint and simplicity between the splendour of the roof and the monumentality of the raised foundations. The columns and walls were typically lacquered and painted in one colour (red in the imperial palaces), which provided a clean and sharp contrast with the polychromatic decoration of the eaves. Only the rhythmic patterns of the delicate window lattice or the studded doors with decorative handles would break up the clean lines and space achieved by the walls and pillars.

Ornamental handles and studs on a ceremonial door in the Forbidden City.

In most cases, the pillars were of pine, but in very special buildings they were made from *nan mu*, a fragrant cedar found in the forests of south-western China. *Nan mu* was costly and even in palace building was used sparingly. The three most memorable buildings built with *nan mu* are the ancestral tablet hall of the Yong Le emperor at the Ming Tombs (see page 142), the halls of the Empress Dowager's tomb at the Eastern Qing Tombs (page 145) and the beautiful Hall of Frugality and Calm in the summer palace resort of Chengde (page 119), commissioned by the Qing emperor Kang Xi. Where *nan mu* was used, paint was not applied to the woodwork which, instead, was carved.

In the later years of the Ming and Qing periods, deforestation and the consequent lack of single large pieces of timber necessitated the practice of making encased or jointed pillars. A single central core of timber would be encased with smaller pieces of timber and bound with iron hoops. The columns would then be covered with hemp and lacquer and it thus became impossible to tell whether the column was a single piece of wood or made up of many segments. However, where a building has yet to be renovated and the lacquer and hemp around the columns have decayed, you can often see the iron bands and wood joints of a fabricated column. In buildings of enormous size with extraordinarily heavy roofs, such as the Drum Tower in Peking, you will often see 'buttressed' columns with two or more columns joined together in order to carry the heavy load of roof timbers.

Columns would typically have been set on stone, or, more rarely, on bronze plinths. These were usually circular and designed to prevent the wood from rotting at its point of contact with the ground. In many buildings in the south of China, where the climate is hotter and damper and the soil holds more moisture, plinths were larger than those in the colder, drier lands of the north. In palace buildings, the plinths were often carved; lotus blossom patterns were particularly popular motifs in the Buddhist-influenced Qing court.

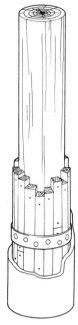

Jointed or encased column.

The Foundations

It was only in the foundations, the third layer in the structural composition of the traditional Chinese building, that the roof found its balance. In the Forbidden City, the three main throne halls, the Hall of Supreme Harmony, the Hall of Preserving Harmony, and the smaller central Hall of Middle Harmony, are set on a three-tiered white stone terrace. (This is often erroneously referred to as marble, but is in fact built of magnesian limestone.) There is a conscious symmetry between the terrace and the building it surrounds with the column caps of the balustrade aligned with the columns of the halls.

These layered terraces are the counterpoint of the grand double roofs of the three halls of state, and without them the buildings would seem top-heavy and lose their lightness of composition. The projecting eaves also help to achieve that lightness of effect: when seen at a distance, the deep shadow cast by the overhanging eaves creates the illusion that the roof floats suspended above the building below.

PEKING -
THE IMPERIAL CITY

The Capital in Dynastic History

Peking became a dynastic capital at only a comparatively late period in imperial Chinese history. Situated in north-east China, it is far from the heartland of early Chinese civilization. The earliest Bronze Age capitals were all sited around the loess-lands in the great bend of the Yellow River, in the region of the present-day provinces of Honan, Shanxi and Shaanxi. In the last province is the most famous of early dynastic capitals, Xi'an, world-renowned as the place where the great army of larger than life model soldiers was unearthed from near the tomb of the first emperor of China, **Qin Shi Huang Di** (reigned 221–210 BC). This city was the first imperial capital of China and it was also later to become the site of the capitals of the **Han** (206 BC–AD 220) and **Tang** (AD 618–907) dynasties. During these two famous eras, Xi'an was known by the poetic name of Changan, meaning 'Eternal Peace'.

However, eternal peace was not to reign in the history of the Chinese empire and the site of the capital was constantly shifted between the north-west, north-east and south-east. The shift between north and south usually took place when a native Chinese dynasty was threatened by an invasion of nomadic warriors from the north. The Great Wall, the earliest sections of which were built during the Zhou dynasty (1122–221 BC), was constructed to keep the northern 'barbarians' out of the settled agrarian heartland of China. However, at uncomfortably frequent intervals in Chinese history, the Wall proved ineffective and nomadic tribes swept southwards to invade, and sometimes conquer and rule, China. In the Song dynasty (AD 960–1279), an invasion from the north led to the abandonment of the northern capital of Kaifeng and the establishment of the capital in the south-eastern city of Hangzhou.

In 1279, the Song were swept away from the south by another invasion from the north, this time by the Mongols.

(Opposite) A stone lion, one of a pair, guarding the entrance to the Imperial City at the Gate of Heavenly Peace.

39

With the conquest of China by the Mongols and the founding of the **Yuan dynasty** (1279–1368), the capital was moved north again. Peking was to replace Hangzhou as a city of imperial splendour. The Yuan was not the first dynasty to use the city as a capital, but it was the first to rule all of China from Peking. The earlier **Liao** and **Jin dynasties** (907–1125 and 1125–1234 respectively), which controlled only the north of China while the Song ruled in the south, had both made Peking their capital and built extensive palaces and fortifications there.

Interestingly, the first three dynasties that used Peking as a capital were all non-native Chinese. But since the dynasties were all founded by nomadic warriors, it is clear that the Liao, Jin and Mongol emperors preferred this north-eastern site because of its proximity to their steppe homelands. It is, after all, only a day's hard ride from Peking to where the grasslands of Central Asia begin and where, by tradition, no Chinese farmer dared venture.

In fact, Peking has been the capital of only one native Chinese dynasty and that was the Ming (1368–1644). However, it was not the choice of the Ming founding emperor, Hong Wu (reigned 1368–98), who made Nanjing, in present-day Jiangsu Province, his capital. This was because he was born in neighbouring Anhui province, had campaigned from the south and had built up a regional power-base from Nanjing thereby putting himself in a position to take all of China from the Mongols.

The move to Peking was made by Hong Wu's son, the Yong Le emperor (reigned 1402–24), who on his father's death in 1398, usurped the throne from his nephew, the Jian Wen (reigned 1399–1402) emperor. The Yong Le emperor, prior to his enthronement, had been the Prince of Yan, (Yan is an old name for the Peking region), and had built up his stronghold in the Peking garrison while guarding the border against further Mongol invasion. The decision by the Yong Le emperor to move his capital to Peking was logical in view of his strong military connections with the region and his perception of the northern frontier as being of the greatest strategic importance in the holding of the empire. The palaces of the Forbidden City that we see today were largely planned and built in the reign of the Yong Le emperor.

After the death of the Yong Le emperor in 1424, his

A portrait of the Ming dynasty Yong Le emperor, architectural patron of imperial Peking.

successor, **Hong Xi** (reigned 1425), decided to move the capital south again to Nanjing. This too would have had its advantages as by this time the provinces around Nanjing and the Yangzi delta were the most prosperous in the country. But the move never took place owing to Hong Xi's early death and the subsequent abandonment of the plan. From then on, Peking was to remain the capital of imperial China.

When the Manchus conquered China in the first half of the seventeenth century, their homeland was in the far north-east, in the area we know as Manchuria and which the Chinese call *Dong Bei* (North East). The Manchu capital, prior to the defeat of the Ming, lay in this region in the city of Shenyang. Because the Manchu overlord **Nurhaci** (reigned 1583–1626) aspired to be the ruler of China, he not only sinicized his court and recruited Chinese troops, he also built a replica palace of the Ming emperors in his own city. But when his grandson, the **Shun Zhi** emperor (reigned 1644–61), went on to defeat the Ming and establish the Qing, the Manchus decided to move their capital to Peking and take up residence in the Ming palaces of the Forbidden City.

Dynastic change usually meant protracted civil war and the inevitable destruction and looting of the palaces of the defeated dynasty. But in 1644, with the suicide of the last Ming emperor **Chong Zhen** (reigned 1628–1644), on the hill to the north of his palace, the Qing army made a swift and largely unopposed move on the Chinese capital, taking the city with relative ease and with little destruction. This was an unusual and fortuitous incident in Chinese history. The beautiful Forbidden City of the Yong Le emperor survived with the minimum of damage, to be reinhabited by a new and foreign imperial house. Thereafter the palaces and all the imperial architecture of Peking were renovated, maintained and extensively rebuilt by a succession of Qing emperors who took very seriously their responsibiity to be true and virtuous 'Sons of Heaven'.

The Design and Development of the Capital

Little of pre-Ming Peking survives in the present layout of the city. However, the waterparks of the first Yuan emperor, **Kubilai Khan** (reigned 1260–94), did survive the upheaval of the civil wars of the fourteenth century when the Ming came to power, and they were to form the basis of the pleasure parks commissioned by the Ming patron of Peking, the Yong Le emperor. Today, those waterparks are known as *Beihai* and *Zhongnanhai*.

The site of the Yuan capital, known as Dadu in Chinese, is to the north of the present city centre. We know that the Yuan city was a regular square in shape, with wide and high whitewashed walls containing three gates on each side. The Yuan city had Drum and Bell Towers which were sited very close to the present Drum and Bell Towers built in the Ming period. (The Yuan towers no longer stand.)

The capital the Yong Le emperor created for himself in Peking was modelled on his father's capital in Nanjing. The city took 14 years to be built and, when finished in 1420, was on a grander scale than its precursor. Also, whereas the hilly terrain of Nanjing had meant that the city walls had had to be built to curve around the contours of the hills and river shore, the flat topography of the site of Peking allowed greater symmetry of design. It was planned and executed as a large walled rectangular city enclosing another walled and moated rectangular 'inner' city of palaces. This inner city, known as the Purple Forbidden City lay on the central north–south axis of Peking, slightly north of centre.

Positioned at the very heart of this inner city were the three principal halls of state of the palace, including the largest and most important hall of the palace, the Hall of Supreme Harmony. Thus, when the emperor sat on his throne in the Hall of Supreme Harmony on the occasion of important state ceremonies, he was both geographically and symbolically at the centre of his capital and, by implication, his empire. The architecture of the capital was therefore of great significance in reflecting the central and divine status of the ruler.

If you look at the map of Peking and follow the central north–south axis of the city, you will notice that most of the major buildings of the capital and Forbidden City lie either directly on that axis or are positioned either side of it. It is also interesting that whereas at the far south of the city there is a southern gate, the Everlasting Stability Gate, *Yong Ding Men*, at the northern limit of the city walls there is no northern gate on the central axis, but rather there are two gates, one to the

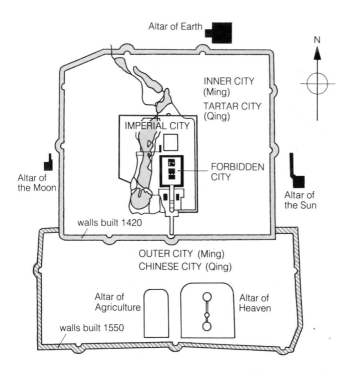

Altar of Earth

INNER CITY
(Ming)

TARTAR CITY
(Qing)

IMPERIAL CITY

N

FORBIDDEN
CITY

Altar of
the Moon

Altar of
the Sun

walls built 1420

OUTER CITY (Ming)
CHINESE CITY (Qing)

Altar of
Agriculture

Altar of
Heaven

walls built 1550

Simple plan to show
main city areas and
suburban altars of
Peking in Ming and
Qing times.

east and one to the west of the central line. This is obviously for reasons of *feng shui* (see pages 8–10).

The central east–west axis of the city known today as Changan Avenue, is not as significant as the north–south line, but the four cardinal points are. The Ming dynasty **Jia Jing** emperor (reigned 1522–66) was the patron of the magnificent suburban altars of the Earth, Sun, Moon and Agriculture in the north, east, west and south of the city respectively. The most important suburban altar, the Altar and Temple of Heaven in the southern suburbs, predates all the other altars, having been built one hundred years earlier, in the Yong Le reign. The Altar and Temple of Agriculture, which lay just to the west of the central southern axis of the city, were torn down in the 1950s to make way for a Worker's Stadium. These altars built on the cardinal points added to the symmetrical balance of the city.

As a pleasant and natural contrast to the symmetrically laid-out palaces, walls, altars and avenues of the capital, the central pleasure parks of the emperors were built in gracefully

(Opposite) Peking under the Ming and Qing
1. Gate of Everlasting Stability, *Yong Ding Men*;
2. Fore Gate, *Qian Men*;
3. Gate of Heavenly Peace, *Tian An Men*;
4. Gate of Correct Deportment, *Duan Men*;
5. Meridian Gate, *Wu Men*;
6. Golden Water Stream, *Jin Shui*;
7. Gate of Supreme Harmony, *Tai He Men*;
8. Halls of Supreme Harmony, *Tai He Dian*, Middle Harmony, *Zhong He Dian*, Preserving Harmony, *Bao He Dian*;
9. Inner palace halls;
10. Prospect Hill, *Jing Shan*;
11. Site of Gate of Earthly Peace, *Di An Men* (northern gate of Imperial City);
12. Drum Tower, *Gu Lou*;
13. Bell Tower, *Zhong Lou*;
14. Imperial Ancestral Temple, *Tai Miao*;
15. Altar to the Soil and Grains, *She Ji Tan*;
16. Imperial Archives, *Huang Shi Cheng*;
17. Altar of Heaven, *Huan Qiu*;
18. Imperial Vault of Heaven, *Huang Qiong Yu*;
19. Hall for Good Harvests, *Qi Nian Dian*;
20. Gate of Peaceful Stability, *An Ding Men*;
21. Gate of Victorious Virtue, *De Sheng Men*;
22. South Lake, *Nanhai*;
23. Central Lake, *Zhonghai*;
24. North Lake, *Beihai*;
25. Temple of Agriculture, *Xian Nong Tan* (demolished 1950s).

asymmetrical settings of curving lakes and tree-studded hills. The bridges, pavilions, towers and open-gallery walkways were carefully designed to create series of set-piece sceneries to be enjoyed from specific vantage points. This was all very different from the grand and awe-inspiring spectacle of the vast courtyards and raised halls of the ceremonial palaces.

Peking, more than any other city in the world we can see today, was the product of a 'grand design' where people and emperor were bound together in an architectural representation of cosmic order. When the emperor stood on the vast, open-air, circular Altar of Heaven at the winter solstice to sacrifice to Heaven, all that he saw above and around him was the sky. For, unlike the European city skyline of tall steeples and spires, Peking's buildings were low and the city was open to the heavens.

That has all changed: the mighty city walls that once girdled the town and defined its space have all been torn down; and when you stand at the centre of the Altar of Heaven all you see around you is a drab ring of tower blocks. It is sometimes hard to imagine the splendour and humanity of old Peking because of the frantic, ugly and much-needed building programme currently underway. But imagine you must, for the splendours of imperial China often seem in danger of being lost or overwhelmed by the sheer number of tourists and the tide of commercialization that engulfs the city. A journey around the architecture of imperial Peking is one that demands vision, sympathy and an understanding of the unkind vicissitudes of Chinese history.

The Imperial City — *Huang Cheng*

In the Ming dynasty, the capital was divided into two distinct areas: the inner city, the original walled rectangle of the grand design and an area to the south known as the outer city, which was only enclosed by walls in the 1550s when the country was again threatened by the Mongols.

In the **Qing** period (1644–1912) these two distinct areas were given different names: the Tartar City and the Chinese City. The Tartar City was the northern inner city section, and the Chinese City, the southern outer district. The reason for this distinction was that as the Manchus had conquered China and

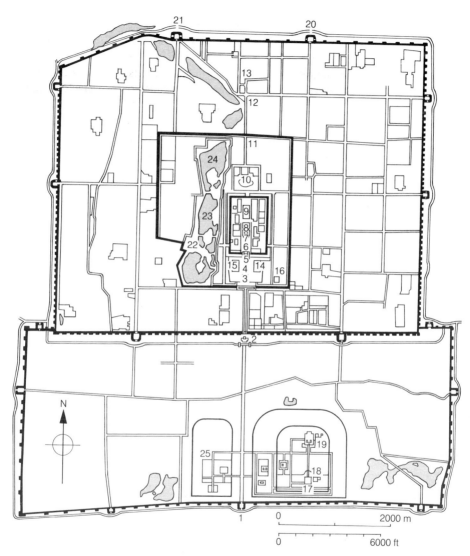

now ruled from the Forbidden City, which lay within the Imperial City in the northern section, Manchu or 'Tartar' princes and nobles lived close to their imperial rulers in the northern district. Chinese officials, whose status was, by policy, kept lower than their Manchu peers, lived in the more distant southern section of the capital.

Within the Tartar City, the Imperial City was the adminis-

45

trative centre of the empire. It was a vast, walled area (most of the walls have since been pulled down), which, in turn, enclosed the Forbidden City, with its own circumference of walls and moat, the lakeside parks and pavilions of *Beihai* and *Zhongnanhai* on the north-west and west, Prospect Hill on the north, and a long strip of land on the eastern side of the Forbidden City. To give some idea of how enormous the original Imperial City once was, it not only enclosed the 72ha (178 acres) of the Forbidden City, its ceremonial and residential centre, but also almost six times that amount of land again in imperial parks, storehouses, official residences, offices and factories.

The important architectural complexes of the Imperial City that survive to this day are: the Forbidden City, which is largely open to visitors; the Imperial Ancestral Temples, open to the public as a Worker's Palace with some of its buildings tastelessly converted for modern usage; the Altar to the Soil and Grains, now converted into a public park; the Imperial Archives, open to the public; Prospect Hill, a public park; *Beihai*, which is also a public park and *Zhongnanhai*, the lakes and halls of which have become the residential and administrative headquarters of China's Communist rulers.

THE FORBIDDEN CITY

In many ways, the physical isolation of the emperor, enclosed by the three great sets of city, Imperial City and Forbidden City walls, was symbolic of his status as a ruler with cosmic status. On many state occasions, the emperor sat behind a screen shrouded in clouds of incense; he was usually carried around the palace in an enclosed sedan chair and many of his officials never set eyes on him. Only the most determined and active emperors, like the Qing dynasty Kang Xi emperor (reigned 1662–1722), escaped this cloistered existence. It is said that he kept his own little black donkey on which he rode around his capital in disguise. The great walls and moat, the labyrinth of courtyards and the screened thrones are testimony to the 'hidden' nature of the emperors' lives. The very name 'Forbidden City' tells much about the difference between the Chinese emperor and a European monarch.

The central palaces of the Imperial City that make up the Forbidden City are known in Chinese as *Zi Jin Cheng*, or

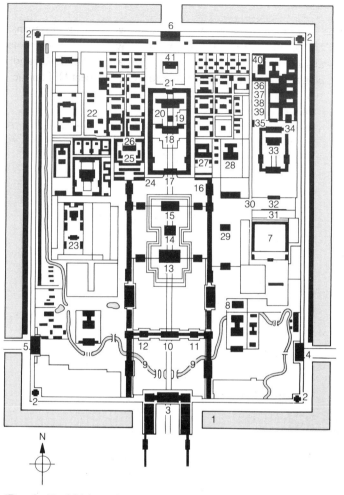

(Plan of Forbidden City cont.)

17. Gate of Heavenly Purity, *Qian Qing Men*; 18. Palace of Heavenly Purity, *Qian Qing Gong*; 19. Hall of Prosperity, *Jiao Tai Dian*; 20. Hall of Earthly Tranquillity, *Kun Ning Gong*; 21. Gate of Earthly Tranquillity, *Kun Ning Men*; 22. Rain Flower Pavilion, *Yu Hua Ge*; 23. Garden of Compassionate Peace, *Ci Ning Hua Yuan*; 24. Inner Left Gate, *Nei Zuo Men*; 25. Nurturing the Heart Gate, *Yang Xin Men*; 26. Nurturing the Heart Hall, *Yang Xin Gong*; 27. Abstinence Hall, *Zhai Gong*; 28. Hall of Offerings to the Ancestors, *Feng Xian Dian*; 29. Archery Ground, *Jian Chang*; 30. Gate of Bestowal of Congratulations, *Xi Qing Men*; 31. Nine Dragon Screen, *Jiu Long Bi*; 32. Imperial Zenith Gate, *Huang Ji Men*; 33. Imperial Zenith Hall, *Huang Ji Dian*; 34. Palace of Peaceful Longevity, *Ning Shou Gong*; 35. Gate of Spreading Happiness, *Yan Qi Men*; 36. Palace Garden of Peaceful Longevity, *Ning Shou Gong Hua Yuan*; 37. Ancient Flowery Porch, *Gu Hua Xuan*; 38. Pavilion of Ceremonial Purification, *Xi Shang Ting*; 39. Three Friends Lodge, *San You Xuan*; 40. Lodge of the Cares of the World, *Juan Qin Zhai*; 41. The Imperial Garden, *Yu Hua Yuan*.

'Purple Forbidden City'. Many people think that the word purple, or *zi*, refers to the claret-coloured walls of the City, but it is in fact derived from a quotation from Confucius. He described the sage ruler as the 'pole star', meaning that such a ruler was a moral example, a constant or a point of reference for human society. The pole star in Chinese is called the *zi wei xing*, the first character of which, *zi*, means purple. Thus the name emphasizes the cosmic and moral significance of the buildings.

In all Chinese imperial architecture, the names of buildings are carefully chosen for their symbolic or literary value, even though they were often changed on the accession of a new dynasty or emperor. Buildings have 'name-boards' over their central entrances inscribed in fine calligraphy, sometimes in the hand of an emperor. (This calligraphic tradition has survived in Communist China with Chairman Mao's calligraphy plastered everywhere from railway stations to the masthead of newspapers!)

In 1403 the Yong Le emperor decided to designate Peking as his new capital and sent his son, the future Hong Xi emperor, to oversee its construction. The capital was built between 1406 and 1420. Thousands of Chinese labourers were drafted into the area to build the palaces, and even craftsmen from as far away as Annam (present-day Vietnam, Laos and Burma) were employed. The chief architect of the Forbidden City was an Annamese eunuch called Ruan An. In 1417, most of the palace buildings were completed. Three years later the Drum and Bell Towers in the north of the city were finished as was the Temple of Heaven to the south. On October 28 1420, Peking officially became the Ming capital. However, in 1421, a fire destroyed the three main palace halls at the centre of the Forbidden City and the emperor called in his officials to criticize his conduct. The scholars denounced the hardships caused by the enormous building programme and, as result, the emperor punished his most vocal critics, had one scholar executed and then had the three halls rebuilt.

Frequent fires were to take a regular toll on the buildings of the Forbidden City. In May 1557, in the Jia Jing reign, the main ceremonial halls burnt down again; they were rebuilt over the following years at the staggering cost of 730,000 ounces of silver. Almost all of the buildings we see in the Forbidden City today date from the Qing period.

The layout of the Forbidden City is strictly symmetrical, except in the residential area of the north-east and north-west, which is a complex maze of halls, courtyards and gardens. Some have criticized the lack of symmetry in the north as being less spatially harmonious than the front and central parts of the city. Personally I find the lack of symmetry in the living quarters of the emperor and his womenfolk reassuringly humane and intimate, a much-needed contrast to the grandeur of the ceremonial and administrative halls.

Before describing individual buildings or areas within the Forbidden City, it might be useful to make some general points about elements and themes in its architecture. Since yellow is the imperial colour of roofs, most of the roofs within the City have yellow tiles. However, there are some exceptions and these are for specific reasons. For example, the Pavilion of Literary Depth, *Wen Yuan Ge*, (which is not currently open to visitors) has black tiles. This building became a library in the reign of the Qing dynasty Qian Long emperor (reigned 1736–95) and black tiles were used on its roof because, in traditional geomancy, black is the corresponding colour of the element of water and would thus help to ward off the danger of fire. In contrast, temples, theatre pavilions and garden architecture have roofs of blue, green, or green and yellow. The Three Southern Residences, *Nan San Suo*, (also not open to visitors) have plain green rather than yellow roofs because the buildings housed the imperial princes.

Roof shape also indicates the status of a building. The hip roof style is always used for the main building in a group. Likewise, the number of the roof guardians on the ends of the

The roof guardians of the Hall of Supreme Harmony. This is the only roof to feature the *xing she* (second from right), a winged demon leaning on a sword.

49

A single entrance doorway featuring relief pattern ceramic tiles and eave and bracket work in ceramic tiles, the Forbidden City.

A baluster cap of the dragon design.

ridges over the eaves varies according to the importance of the building. Twelve is the highest number, found only on the Hall of Supreme Harmony, the main throne hall of the City. Other buildings can have three, five, seven or nine figures. They are always, with the exception of the Hall of Supreme Harmony, set out in odd numbers, because odd numbers are *yang*, or of the male or dominant principle. Even numbers are *yin*, and therefore feminine or passive. Because *yang* is 'male', its symbols are suitable for the emperor and his buildings.

The importance of *yang* numbers in palace buildings is evident even in the number of nails studded in the great door panels of the gates. The gates of the emperor are studded with nine times nine rows giving the *yang* number of 81. This number is significant as nine is the number that represents Heaven. Only the gates used by the emperor could have 81 nails; lesser gates for officials had 49 (seven times seven) or 25 (five times five). The only exception to this rule of *yang* numbers is the Eastern Floral Gate, which has the *yin* number of 72 (nine times eight) nails. Many stories are told to explain why this should be so, but the most interesting relates that as it was the gate through which the emperor's corpse was taken on the way to the imperial mausoleum, it was fitting that the doors should have a *yin* number of nails — funerals are a *yin* occasion because they involve the return of a body to the earth.

Even the stone baluster caps on the terraces of the Forbidden City are set out according to the nature of the building or bridge they frame. Look carefully at the five bridges over the Golden Water stream between the Meridian Gate and the Gate of Supreme Harmony, and you will see that the central bridge, used only by the emperor, has dragon and cloud caps. The auxiliary bridges have flame-shaped caps symbolizing the Twenty Four Solar Terms; the key dates in the lunar calendar, by which the agricultural cycle was ordered. In the gardens, more decorative baluster caps are used; these can be square, pomegranate-shaped, lotus-shaped or phoenix-patterned. Around the most important throne halls, baluster caps are dragon- and phoenix-patterned, the two animals together symbolizing the emperor and empress.

* * *

The whole of the Forbidden City is set within a moated and

walled rectangle 7550m (2,460ft) wide from east to west and 960m (3,150ft) long from north to south. The design is dominated by the central north–south axis along which only the emperor could pass. His thrones were set on the line of the axis and only he, except on rare occasions when an empress was officially welcomed, could move through the central gates. Officials had to pass through auxiliary gates to the east and west of the centre. The **wall** surrounding the Forbidden City is 10m (32ft) high with four towers that stand above the walls at each corner. The **corner towers** were not built for defensive reasons (the outer city walls had massive masonry towers for that purpose); instead, they are highly complex decorative structures built to be admired from beyond the walls by outsiders. They are built on a stepped square-cross plan and have lower walls of brick surmounted by lattice panels. It is the roofs which are of most interest, each tower having a complex set of three layers of eaves which have 72 separate roof ridges. The upper roof eaves form a set of four hip-and-gables, topped with a central golden finial and four dragon acroteria. The two lower layers of eaves are four sets of interlocking hip-and-gable roofs. Seen from a distance, the towers have a shape reminiscent of castles in Japan, where the gable end is a focus of the composition of the buildings. In Chinese architecture, the gable end is seldom placed at the centre of the composition.

The **moat** encircling the walls is 52m (170ft) wide and has the virtue of acting as a mirror to the broad red walls of the City.

A baluster cap of the phoenix design.

Corner tower and moat of the Forbidden City.

* * *

Gates in Chinese architecture are not quite the simple affairs that they often are in western architecture. The Chinese gate is frequently a building or set of buildings in itself. The Forbidden City has four gates, but can now only be entered from the south through the Meridian Gate, *Wu Men*. The two gates to the south of the Meridian Gate, the Gate of Heavenly Peace, *Tian An Men*, and the Gate of Correct Deportment, *Duan Men*, are not actually part of the Forbidden City proper. The side gate to the east, known as the Eastern Floral Gate, *Dong Hua Men*, which was the traditional ceremonial entrance of the emperor's civil officials, is open and leads into the great courtyard to the south of the Meridian Gate. The Western Floral Gate, *Xi Hua Men*, once used as the entrance for military officials, is closed. Up until recently, visitors could also enter through the north Gate of Martial Spirit, *Shen Wu Men*, but the sheer volume of visitors has taken such a toll on the fabric of the buildings, that in an attempt to control numbers, sightseers are now allowed to approach the palaces only from the south. In fact, many of the Forbidden City's 8,700 halls and buildings are still off-limits because they are either derelict or

The Gate of Heavenly Peace flanked by stone lions and *hua biao*, the dragon-carved state totem.

are being used for storage and living quarters for staff.

The **Gate of Heavenly Peace**, *Tian An Men*, was the main entrance to the Imperial City. It is through this gate that the main entrance of the Forbidden City, the Meridian Gate, is approached. It is a walled gate with a hall set above the centre. The hall is a double-eaved, hip-and-gable roofed building, nine bays wide. Below the hall are five barrel-vault tunnel entrances, the central one of which is the largest. It was this central gate that only the emperor could use — officials used the four flanking gates. This gate has become one of the modern symbols of Peking because it overlooks the wide-open space of *Tian An Men* Square, a famous venue for present-day political rallies. However, in imperial times, there was no square here, but only a wide north–south thoroughfare leading straight to the Fore Gate *Qian Men* (see p.98). Either side of the thoroughfare stood offices. For example, in the Qing dynasty, the palace hospital was just to the south-east of the Gate of Heavenly Peace. The gate itself was only used for high ceremonial occasions such as the worship of the spirit of the road when the emperor despatched an army to war, the delivery of an imperial proclamation or during a procession by the emperor to a sacrifice at the Temple of Heaven.

The two pairs of white stone columns on either side of the Gate of Heavenly Peace to the north and south are forms of state totems known as *hua biao*. The columns are sculpted with the form of a writhing dragon and at the top have a decorative winged panel in cloud relief. Above this sits a *hou*, a mythical creature who is there, it was said, to oversee and report to the emperor. The two beasts to the north of the gate look into the palace and have their mouths closed. The pair to the south have their mouths open and were said to summon the emperor back to the palace if he was needed when away on tour.

The two carved stone lions flanking the southern central entrance of the Gate of Heavenly Peace are also important symbols in imperial architecture, for they represent the power and authority of the emperor. They are believed to date back to the Ming period. The lion on the right, or east, is male and has an ornamental ball under his paw. The lion on the left, to the west, is female and has a cub playfully tipped upside down under her paw. Legend has it that the female has no nipples so the cub must suckle from her paw!

THE OUTER COURT — *Wai Chao*

The city is divided into two distinct areas: the Outer Court and the Inner Court. All of the city south of the Gate of Heavenly Purity, *Qian Qing Men*, is the Outer Court; all the buildings to the north are within the Inner Court. Buildings of the Outer Court all had a ceremonial, administrative or educational function, whereas most of the buildings in the Inner Court were residential or for informal entertaining.

The **Meridian Gate**, *Wu Men*, which is the main entrance to the Forbidden City, also marks the southern boundary of the Outer Court. It is the most imposing and largest walled gate of the Forbidden City. Like the Gate of Heavenly Peace, it has five tunnel entrances but its distinctive walls are set in an impressive square-edged 'U' shape, facing south. On the top of the walls are a central hall with a double-eaved hip roof and four, square, corner pavilions also with double eaves. Each of the four pavilions is topped with a golden ball finial. It was from the Meridian Gate that the emperor announced the new calendar and celebrated military victories. In the Ming dynasty, the courtyard in front of the gate was the site for the flogging of officials who had offended the emperor or any of his favourite eunuchs. In the absence of the emperor, court audiences were held in front of this gate under the supervision

European illustration of a Qing dynasty ceremony taking place in the great courtyard in front of the Meridian Gate, the Forbidden City.

The Golden Water, the stream which is brought through the courtyard in front of the Gate of Supreme Harmony in the shape of an archery bow, the Forbidden City.

of imperial princes or grand secretaries. The gate was built in the reign of the Yong Le emperor and extensively restored in the reign of the first Qing emperor, Shun Zhi (reigned 1644–61). It is sometimes known as the Five Phoenix Tower because of its five buildings set above the walls.

Entering through the dark tunnel of the Meridian Gate, one sees ahead a blaze of brilliant light. This is because the gate leads directly out into a vast courtyard, the space of which is broken by the **Golden Water**, *Jin Shui*, a stream with five bridges. This juxtaposition of light and dark, space and solid shapes, is an important feature of Chinese architecture and is well illustrated in the contrasts of buildings, gates and courtyards in the Forbidden City. The five white stone bridges are low-arched and do not break the rhythm of the space of the courtyard. The Golden Water flows into the courtyard from west to east and is channelled from the lake at *Beihai* (see page 106). The stream is brought round the centre of the courtyard in the shape of an archery bow and its five bridges represent the five Confucian virtues of humanity, sense of duty, wisdom,

A bronze lion, one of a pair, outside the Gate of Supreme Harmony. This is the female with a cub tipped upside down beneath her paw, the Forbidden City.

reliability and ceremonial propriety. The movement of the water in front of the main gate before the ceremonial palaces is geomantically significant and was believed to be auspicious.

The grandeur of the **Gate of Supreme Harmony**, *Tai He Men*, emphasizes its importance as the main entrance to the central courtyard of the City. It is the largest freestanding gate of the city (the higher ones are walled gates) and rests on a single-tier stone terrace as a hall with a double-eaved hip-and-gable roof. Standing in front are the two grandest bronze lions of the palace. To its sides, linked by an adjoining wall, are two auxiliary gates with their own names: to the east is the **Gate of Luminous Virtue**, *Zhao De Men*, used for civil officials; to the west is the **Gate of Correct Conduct**, the *Zheng Du Men*, for military officials. It was at the Gate of Supreme Harmony, in 1644, that the first emperor of the Qing dynasty, Shun Zhi, ascended the throne. Enthronements usually took place in the throne room, the Hall of Supreme Harmony, but on the defeat of the Ming dynasty the main throne room had been destroyed and the gate hall was used instead.

Set on a three-tiered white stone terrace shaped like the letter 'H' set on its side, the **three main ceremonial halls** of the Outer Court are the most important state buildings of the Forbidden City. From south to north, the first and largest is the Hall of Supreme Harmony; the second is the Hall of Middle Harmony; and the third is the Hall of Preserving Harmony. The grand three-tiered terrace on which they stand is referred to as the **Dragon Pavement**.

Set to the north and south of the Dragon Pavement are carved sloping ramps, over which the emperor was carried in his sedan chair. These ramps are known as imperial carriageways. Imperial carriageways can be found in front of other important halls throughout the Forbidden City, but those of the three halls of state are the most impressive with their imperial theme of pearl-chasing dragons amid clouds, wave-filled seas and mountains. The dragon is the common motif for the imperial carriageways leading to ceremonial buildings, but look out for other motifs in front of less important buildings. The imperial carriageway to the north of the Dragon Pavement leading down from the Hall of Preserving Harmony, is a three-tiered ramp of 16.57m (54ft), said to weigh 250 tons. It has an impressive pattern of paired and single front-facing dragons with their bodies weaving in and out of the clouds. The carriageway dates from the Ming dynasty but was recarved in the reign of the Qian Long emperor.

An imperial carriageway featuring dragons amidst foaming seas and clouds.

The **Hall of Supreme Harmony**, *Tai He Dian*, is the most important and largest of the three halls of state. Its present structure dates from the Qing dynasty as does its name. Like many other buildings throughout the Forbidden City, its name has been changed from its Ming original, which was the Hall of Offering to Heaven, *Feng Tian Dian*. This is also the largest building in the Forbidden City, standing at 28m (91ft) above the Dragon Pavement. It is 64m (209ft) wide and 37m (121ft) deep with a massive floor space of 2,380m^2 (25,000ft^2) that has not been divided in the interior except for two narrow side corridors. The grandness of the open interior is emphasized by the large circular inner roof columns arranged in three

(Above) The Hall of Supreme Harmony, the largest and most important ceremonial building of the Forbidden City.

(Below) A bronze sculpture of a turtle on the Dragon Pavement in front of the Hall of Supreme Harmony, the Forbidden City.

transverse lines. The building is set out in 11 bays and has a double-eaved hip roof.

An interesting and easily overlooked feature of the roof of this hall is the extra roof guardian set up above the eaves' ridge. This winged figure, of a man with a monster's face leaning against a sword, is known as the *xing she* and is not found on any other roof in Chinese imperial architecture. Its origins and significance, like many other symbols in Chinese architecture, are now the subject of conjecture. What one cannot overlook in the Hall of Supreme Harmony is the magnificent 'lantern' ceiling set above the throne. The timbers rise above a square frame in a sequence of octagons, squares and circles. In the cupola at the centre is a gilded dragon with silver mirror balls suspended from its mouth to represent pearls. The pearl is one of the eight precious jewels in Chinese tradition and signifies purity. Magic pearls were also believed to shine in the dark. The theme of the dragon is omnipresent in Chinese palace architecture. For example, in this hall the dragon theme is repeated on the painted panels of the woodwork, the six gilded pillars around the throne, the ceiling panels and the carving of the throne itself. Even the robes worn by the emperor on the throne were embroidered with patterns of dragons. The dragons associated with the emperor have five claws, those featured on non-imperial architecture always have less than five.

The dragon was not the only animal to feature as a motif in imperial ceremony. Outside the Hall of Supreme Harmony, on the south section of the Dragon Pavement, are two pairs of bronze animal sculptures: the dragon-headed tortoise and the crane. They are both symbols of longevity and the tortoise is often depicted as the animal who carries official stone tablet inscriptions (see page 155). Also outside the front of the Hall of Supreme Harmony are two important emblems of imperial authority: the sundial, on the east side, and a bronze weight, the *liang*, which was the standard measure for grain, set on a stone pedestal on the west. They symbolized the emperor's authority to regulate time and measure.

The ceremony of the emperor's enthronement took place in the Hall of Supreme Harmony. It was here too that grand court audiences were conducted, the emperor marked the winter solstice, celebrated the lunar New Year and received congratulations on his birthday. All these ceremonies involved the marking of time: when the emperor ascended the throne, a new era of reign would begin. The ability of the emperor to keep good order was symbolized by his regulation of the seasons.

A bronze sculpture of a crane on the Dragon Pavement in front of the Hall of Supreme Harmony, the Forbidden City.

The **Hall of Middle Harmony**, *Zhong He Dian*, the second throne hall, is believed to be the hall closest to its original structural design. It has a lightness of composition which is a pleasant contrast to the heavier structures either side. Only 256 metres square (2752ft²), its lightness of form is a result of an open colonnade on all four sides and long lattice window and door panels on all wall surfaces, which allow light to penetrate right through the building and seem to release the roof from the ground. There are only a few buildings in the Forbidden City that use latticework to such good effect.

The Hall of Middle Harmony was used as an antechamber where the emperor prepared himself before important ceremonies or sacrifices. It was here that he inspected the implements before the spring ploughing ceremony held at the Altar of Agriculture in the southern suburbs. The hall has a lantern ceiling, under which the emperor was believed able to commune with Heaven. The throne in this hall is attractively plain. The extraordinarily polished floor of this and the other two halls of state is the result of the prolonged baking of the floor bricks which have been treated with tung oil. This brown oil comes from the tung, or Chinese wood-oil tree, *Alevrites fordii*.

The **Hall of Preserving Harmony**, *Bao He Dian*, is the rear hall of the three and balances the composition with its hip-and-gable roof set with double eaves. It is smaller than the Hall of Supreme Harmony, at a height of only 22m (72ft). The gable-end decoration of this building is a beautiful configuration of gold-painted relief-carved designs of interlocking circles and fluttering ribbons. This form of gable decoration is an often-missed feature because Chinese buildings were not designed to be viewed from the side. However, it is worth walking to the side of hip-and-gable roof buildings to look at the gable-end

The Hall of Preserving Harmony seen from the north, the Forbidden City.

decorations. The gold relief pattern of circles and ribbons is a feature of imperial architecture and can vary in complexity according to the size and importance of the building.

This hall was also a throne room and used for ceremonial and administrative functions. Foreign embassies were entertained here. However, once every three years it became an examination hall for the top civil service candidates who were graded to take the imperial examination. In this examination, the emperor himself could set the papers and candidates would be received in person by their sovereign.

THE INNER COURT — *Nei Chao*

Behind the Hall of Preserving Harmony is a back courtyard area with gates to the north, east and west. The western gate is sealed and the palaces and gardens beyond are not yet open to view. The gate to the east, the Gate of Prospect and Fortune, *Jing Yun Men*, leads into the north-eastern section of the Forbidden City. The northern gate, the Gate of Heavenly Purity, marks the boundary between the Outer and Inner Courts. Behind this gate, on the central axis line, lie the Three Inner Palaces which in their composition echo, on a smaller scale, the Three Halls of State in the Outer Court.

The **Gate of Heavenly Purity**, *Qian Qing Men*, is a single-eaved, hip-and-gable building of five bays. The three central bays are open and at the centre of their floor space are the gates. The two side bays of the building have been enclosed to form rooms. It was at this gate, in the Qing dynasty, that the court ran its foreign affairs office to deal with foreigners. The office was known as the *yamen.* Two bronze lions flank the central set of steps in front of the gate. This gate is believed to be the least renovated of all the palace gates and must in its present form closely resemble its original Ming structure.

The **Three Inner Palaces**, *Hou San Gong*, are the Palace of Heavenly Purity, *Qian Qing Gong*; the Hall of Prosperity, *Jiao Tai Dian*, and the Hall of Earthly Tranquillity, *Kun Ning Gong*. The names of the south and north palaces, the *Qian Qing Gong* and *Kun Ning Gong*, are linked by the symbolism of the divination lines of the *Yi Jing* divination text (see page 36): *qian* is the trigram of three unbroken lines that represents the *yang* principle and the south: *kun* is the trigram of three broken lines that represents *yin* and the north. During the Ming dynasty the

The Palace of Heavenly Purity, the main palace of the Inner Court of the Forbidden City.

south palace was the residence of the emperor and the north palace the residence of the empress. Thus the male/female, north/south principles are reflected in the conscious contrast of the names. The central hall, *Jiao Tai Dian*, also has a significant name but one which refers to a classical quotation '*tian di jiao tai*', meaning that the fusion of Heaven and Earth is productive.

The Three Inner Palaces are not as grand in scale as the Three Halls of State of the Outer Court and are raised above only a single-tier stone terrace, whereas the halls of the Outer Court are on a three-tiered terrace. The imperial carriageway, the carved stone ramp in front of the halls, depicts the dragon and phoenix together, the dual symbol of emperor and empress.

The major building of the three, the **Palace of Heavenly Purity**, has a double-eaved hip roof. The motifs of the painted panels of this palace are all dragons. Above the throne is an inscribed board with the characters '*zheng da guang ming*' — an exhortation to the sovereign to be upright, great, illustrious and brilliant!

The **Hall of Prosperity**, to the rear of the Palace of Heavenly Purity, echoes the Hall of Middle Harmony in the Outer Court in its square form and single-eaved roof with central gilded finial. However, it has none of the lightness or elegance of the

Hall of Middle Harmony. The solid masonry walls with inset door panels and window lattice give a heavier feel to the building. Within is an enormous water clock and the empty cases of the imperial seals. The hall was used by the empresses as their throne room and the dominant painted motif of this hall is the phoenix, symbol of the empress. Above the throne is an inscription board with the great Daoist maxim *wu wei*, meaning 'inactivity' (see page 14).

The rear building, the **Hall of Earthly Tranquillity** does not have a hip-and-gable roof even though it is the corresponding building to the hip-and-gable-roofed Hall of Preserving Harmony in the Outer Court. Instead it has a double-eaved hip roof, which signifies its original importance as the residence of the empress in the Ming period. In the Qing dynasty, empresses no longer resided here but used it as a state room for their own ceremonies. It was here that the shamanistic secret ceremonies of the Manchus were performed, well away from the disapproving gaze of Confucian Chinese officials. The hall was also used as the imperial nuptial chamber by many of the Qing emperors. In keeping with its intimate functions, its interior has been divided into a set of rooms and is totally unlike the open interiors of the halls of the Outer Court. The dominant colour of the interior paintwork is red, the colour used for Chinese weddings. The last emperor of China was supposed to have spent his wedding night here in 1922, but fled the building later saying that its interior resembled a melted red wax candle!

The roof of the Rain Flower Pavilion with gilt bronze flood dragons.

THE NORTH-WESTERN PALACES OF THE INNER COURT

The north-western section of the Inner Court was the residential area of emperors, and has some of the finest architecture of the Forbidden City. Unfortunately, very little of it is open to visitors. However, standing at a high point in the City, you can see to the north-west the distinctive roof of the **Rain Flower Pavilion**, *Yu Hua Ge*. This particularly fine roof has four gilt-bronze flood dragons set at the corners of the ridges of the upper eaves. The building was used for Buddhist worship and its central finial is a Buddhist stupa. Its roof design is complex, with a lower set of eaves set out in a square form with two convex-ridged porticoes to the north and south.

The Approaching Light Left Gate marking a long alleyway to the west of the main courtyard of the Inner Court; this marks the boundary of the northwestern area of the Forbidden City.

The tiles of the lower level eaves are green with a yellow rim. The next layer is a hip-and-gable roof over a rectangular hall with gallery. Here the tiles are yellow with a blue rim. The top part of the pavilion is a square tower with an open walkway. Above this upper section is a plain yellow roof with the flood dragons at the four corners of the eaves and the central Buddhist emblem of a stupa.

Also in the north-western quarter is the beautiful Garden of Compassionate Peace, *Ci Ning Hua Yuan*, which is, unfortunately, not open to visitors either. The other garden of the north-west, the Establishing Happiness Palace Garden, *Jian Fu Gong Hua Yuan*, commissioned by the Qian Long emperor in the 18th century, is likewise off-limits and lies, sadly, in ruins.

The residential compound of the Qing emperors, the Palace of Nurturing the Heart, is one of the few compounds of the north-western quarter open to view. The palace is entered through the **Inner Left Gate**, *Nei Zuo Men*, to the north-west of the Hall of Preserving Harmony in the Outer Court. This small gate is typical of many of the minor gates of the Forbidden City, with its small tiled eaves, decorative tiled wall panels with raised flower motifs either side of the entrance, and mock beam-and-bracket work in green and yellow tiles.

The **Palace of Nurturing the Heart**, *Yang Xin Gong*, lies west of the Inner Left Gate, its buildings arranged around a double courtyard. This palace compound best exemplifies the ordered intimacy of Chinese residential buildings. The halls and courtyards, built to be the residential area of the emperor of China, have little of the grandeur of the ceremonial buildings of the Outer Court. The bronze lions flanking the main gate of the complex, the **Nurturing the Heart Gate**, *Yang Xin Men*, are small in scale but of very fine craftsmanship. The gate itself has a single entrance with decorative panels of tiles sculpted with flower and bird designs. In front of the gate stands a carved jade disc on a stone pedestal. The jade disc, or *bi*, has represented the power of the ruler in China since the Bronze Age; such jade discs were frequently buried with the corpses of rulers and nobles.

Inside the gate is a free-standing red wooden gate with tiled eaves. The closed door panels act effectively as a 'spirit screen' (see page 26). The main hall of the complex, the **Nurturing the Heart Hall**, *Yang Xin Dian*, is divided into living rooms and

bedchambers. However, at the centre of the hall is a throne and writing table where the emperor worked. Above the throne is an inscription board with the characters '*zhong zheng ren he*', meaning central, upright, sincere and harmonious. Even within the emperor's own living quarters, the burden of imperial virtue was made a theme of interior design! In fact, the name of the hall itself comes from a quotation from Mencius exhorting the ruler to be virtuous in his government.

The jade disc in front of the Nurturing the Heart Gate, the gate to the residential quarters of the Qing emperors in the Forbidden City.

THE NORTH-EASTERN PALACES OF THE INNER COURT

The **north-eastern section** of the Inner Court is where most of the permanent and temporary exhibitions of the Palace Museum are put on display and is thus largely open to visitors. Buildings in this quarter include the residences of the imperial concubines, the Abstinence Hall, *Zhai Gong*, where the emperor fasted before sacrifices and ceremonies of cosmic significance, the Hall of Offerings to the Ancestors, *Feng Xian Dian*, and the Palace and Garden of Peaceful Longevity. The palace and garden were commissioned by the Qian Long emperor in the 18th century for his retirement, and it is these palaces and garden buildings that will be described in this section.

In 1796, the Qian Long emperor abdicated out of filial respect for his grandfather, the Kang Xi emperor. Kang Xi had ruled for 60 years, and the Qian Long emperor, remembering the kindness and attention paid to him by his grandfather, decided that he too should not reign for more than 60 years. Thus, in preparation for his retirement, he had a special palace compound renovated, and he commissioned a new garden. His choice of name for the palace and garden, Peaceful Longevity, reflected his desire to detach himself from the affairs of state. In reality, Qian Long spent little time in this palace after his abdication and could not resist the temptation to take decisions for his son, the **Jia Qing** emperor (reigned 1796–1820), who was himself already in his sixties!

In order to visit the Palace and Garden of Peaceful Longevity, you have to leave the rear courtyard of the Three Halls of State through the north-east gate, the Gate of Prospect and Fortune, *Jing Yun Men* and walk across the northern part of the Archery Ground, *Jian Chang*. You then must pass through the small Gate of Bestowal of Congratulations, *Xi Qing Men* before you reach the main gate that leads into the Palace of Peaceful Longevity, the **Imperial Zenith Gate**, *Huang Ji Men*, which is on your left. On your right, to the south of the gate, is the wonderful **Nine Dragon Screen**, *Jiu Long Bi*, of polychromatic glazed tiles. This was built in 1771 in the Qian Long era and depicts nine (the number of Heaven) different coloured dragons playing amidst the waves. The central dragon faces forward and the other eight are in profile. The screen is more than 29.4m (96ft) long and 3.5m (11ft) high. It is crowned with a small yellow-tiled, single-eaved roof, the ridge of which has a highly decorative frieze of tiles sculpted with green dragons in yellow clouds.

The two main buildings of the **Palace of Peaceful Longevity**, *Ning Shou Gong* — the **Imperial Zenith Hall**, *Huang Ji Dian*, and the palace itself — were modelled on the Palace of Heavenly Purity and Palace of Earthly Tranquillity respectively. They are both grand ceremonial buildings set on a single-tier white stone terrace. The decorative theme of these buildings is the dragon and phoenix together, which appears also on the baluster caps of the terrace balustrade, the painted

panels of the woodwork and in the carving of the imperial carriageway in front of the Imperial Zenith Hall. This stone ramp is exceptional for having its design set into geometrical panels. The magnificent central dragon is contained in a curving leaf-patterned border arranged within a star which is set inside an octagon. In the four corners are phoenixes with their wings outstretched. The background pattern is of interlocking hexagons framing flowers. It is an unusually complex and finely-wrought imperial carriageway.

However, it is in the garden that Qian Long created for his retirement that he surpassed himself in architectural whimsy and grandeur. The **Palace Garden of Peaceful Longevity**, *Ning Shou Gong Hua Yuan*, is entered from the south through the **Gate of Spreading Happiness**, *Yan Qi Men*, a small, unpretentious structure with a single-eaved flush gable roof and one central entrance. The gate leads straight into a massive rockery designed to give an air of mystery and anticipation as you enter.

The garden is a long, narrow rectangle which runs from

The Imperial Zenith Hall in the Palace of Peaceful Longevity complex in the north-eastern section of the Forbidden City.

north to south, with an area of just less than 6,000m² (64,000ft²). It is divided into four sections and has none of the symmetry of the Imperial Garden. Three out of the four garden areas have massive rockeries which are the outstanding feature of this garden complex. These rockeries have been very carefully devised, often imitating styles of rocks in paintings. They are very different from the European idea of a rockery and are more like the Gothic grotto seen in some 18th-century English country parks.

The main hall of the first southern section of the garden, the **Ancient Flowery Porch**, *Gu Hua Xuan*, is a fine example of studied simplicity, a quality much admired in Chinese garden architecture. It is a plain rectangular structure with no enclosing walls. Its roof is a simple, single-eaved, hip-and-gable form with the pleasing convex roof ridge that is a common feature of garden architecture. Delicate latticework frames the columns and lintels, and the unpainted ceiling panels of *nan mu* (a fragrant cedarwood from south China) have elegant carved reliefs of intertwined flowers. From within, the open columns framed with latticework give a series of varied vistas of ancient trees, layered rocks and other garden buildings.

One of the buildings to be seen from the Ancient Flowery Porch is the **Pavilion of Ceremonial Purification**, *Xi Shang Ting*, in the south-west corner of the garden. The pavilion is built on a 'T'-shaped plan, with the main section of the building

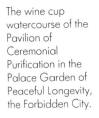

The wine cup watercourse of the Pavilion of Ceremonial Purification in the Palace Garden of Peaceful Longevity, the Forbidden City.

enclosed by wooden walls and latticework panels; an open portico leads out from the enclosed frame. Around the portico is a low, white stone wall with bamboo motifs, and baluster rails and caps sculpted in the form of folded bamboo stems. However, what is exceptional about the pavilion is the stone floor of its portico, which has been carved into a watercourse in the shape of the '*ru yi*' symbol (this is the symbol of 'whatsoever you desire'). The watercourse was used for floating wine cups during poetry recitations and drinking sessions held by the emperor for his closest friends. Other such wine cup streams exist elsewhere in imperial architecture: there is one in a garden of the Forbidden City that is closed to visitors, and another in *Zhongnanhai*.

Other interesting details of the pavilion exemplify architectural themes in garden building. For example, the delicate latticework has the popular bat-shaped 'knuckles', which hold lattice frames in place — bats are the symbol of happiness in Chinese iconography. Look up at the painted panels on the roof timbers in this pavilion and you will see attractive landscape vignettes painted in the '*Su shi*' style (see page 21). The unhewn natural rock steps that lead up to the pavilion are also a common and much-loved feature of Chinese garden architecture.

In the third section of the garden is the **Three Friends Lodge**, *San You Xuan*, which is almost a pattern book for the design motifs of the garden. In Chinese art, the 'Three Friends' refer to the bamboo, plum and pine; they symbolize constancy in inclement weather because all three either stay green or flower in the cold season. The Qian Long emperor took the 'Three Friends' as the emblem motif of his whole garden, and this building in particular, because they were suitable symbols for the winter of his life. In this lodge, all the design details feature these three plants; other buildings throughout the garden also feature one or more of the plants as a central or secondary motif.

The Lodge of the Cares of the World in the Palace Garden of Peaceful Longevity.

Perhaps one of the most arresting and picturesque interiors of any palace building is to be found in this garden, in the northernmost section, in the **Lodge of the Cares of the World**, *Juan Qin Zhai*. A small theatre stage is the focus of its interior and opposite the stage is a partitioned recess and gallery of fine and intricate woodwork. But what is remarkable about the

The Imperial Garden
Plan, *Yu Hua Yuan*
1. Hall of Imperial
Tranquillity, *Qin An
Dian*;
2. Ten Thousand
Springs Pavilion, *Wan
Chun Ting*;
3. Thousand Autumns
Pavilion, *Qian Qiu
Ting*;
4. Floating Jade
Pavilion, *Fu Bi Ting*;
5. Auspicious Clarity
Pavilion, *Cheng Rui
Ting*;
6. Pavilion of Imperial
View, *Yu Jing Ting*;
7. Hall of Pears and
Pondweed, *Li Cao
Tang*.

setting are the *trompe l'oeil* paintings on the walls and ceiling. Chinese artisans were skilled painters of *trompe l'oeil* on the woodwork of buildings; many garden pavilions have charming paintings of decorative objects such as flower vases and lutes which seem to balance delicately in mid-air. However, what is rare in Chinese architecture is to find a *trompe l'oeil* painting on such a grand scale. In this building, the walls on either side of the stage create a backdrop of buildings and above is a wonderful fresco of a trellis heavy with wistaria blossom. The total effect is one of light-hearted charm and it is easy to understand why the emperor chose such a name for his retreat from the cares of statecraft.

THE IMPERIAL GARDEN — *Yu Hua Yuan*

In imperial times, there were four gardens in the Forbidden City of which three survive. The Imperial Garden lies directly to the north of the Three Inner Palaces. It is the oldest and was landscaped in the Yong Le reign during the initial phase of palace building completed in 1420. Many of its juniper trees date back to this period. The garden covers just over 11,000m² (13,200yd²) and is notable for its symmetry, an unusual feature

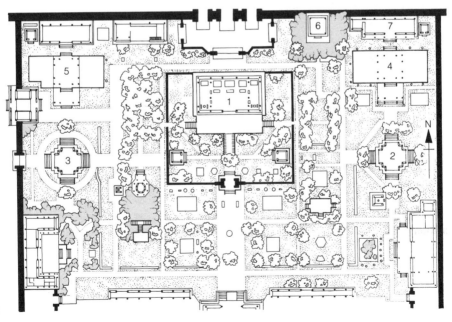

for a Chinese garden. To the north of centre is the main hall of the garden, the Hall of Imperial Tranquillity. Two large double-eaved pavilions, the Ten Thousand Springs Pavilion and the Thousand Autumns Pavilion, stand to east and west. Two, smaller, single-eaved pavilions with porticoes lie in the north-east and north-west of the garden, and auxiliary halls, pavilions and lodges are sited along the eastern, northern and western walls of the garden. This symmetry is softened by the clever disposition of trees, rockeries, dividing walls and the diversity of building shape, size and roof style.

The **Hall of Imperial Tranquillity**, *Qin An Dian*, is the only original Ming building of the Forbidden City to stand untouched by later renovation. It was used as a temple in imperial times and its central roof ornament, a Buddhist stupa, indicates its religious function. The roof is an interesting and unusual structure as it has no central roof ridge; instead, there is a flat rectangular terrace in the middle of the top set of eaves. The roof is built in the double-eaved hip style and the proportion of the two sets of eaves indicates its Ming origins: later Qing buildings tend to have dominant upper eaves, with the lower set of eaves overshadowed, but the roof of this building has well-balanced upper and lower eaves.

The two major pairs of pavilions, the **Ten Thousand Springs Pavilion**, *Wan Chun Ting*, on the east, and the **Thousand Autumns Pavilion**, *Qian Qiu Ting*, on the west, have a wonderful design. The lower structure and eaves are built on a stepped square-cross form with a circular upper roof. Even the names of these pavilions have a symmetry, for the corresponding direction of spring is east and that of autumn is the west. (There is nothing accidental or haphazard in the landscaping of a Chinese garden, the composition of its architecture or the naming of its buildings.)

The symmetry of these pavilions is echoed in the siting of the two smaller pavilions, the **Floating Jade Pavilion**, *Fu Bi Ting*, in the north-east of the garden, and the **Auspicious Clarity Pavilion**, *Cheng Rui Ting*, in the north-west. They are both built over pools which would have been stocked with fish and waterlilies. They are single-eaved buildings with a square open frame, linked to a rectangular portico. All these pavilions would have been used for entertainment, whether for drinking tea or merely for gazing at the fish in the water.

In the north-east of the garden is a massive rockery which is topped with a square pavilion with a blue and yellow roof. This is the **Pavilion of Imperial View**, *Yu Jing Ting*, which gives an excellent view over the garden and roofs of the palace as well as to the lakeside parks and distant western hills beyond Peking. Next to it stands the **Hall of Pears and Pondweed**, *Li Cao Tang*, where the Qian Long emperor kept his most precious books. Again, it is no accident that an emperor kept a special library in his garden retreat. Gardens were a popular place for literary entertainments and such books would be better stored close at hand for poetry-writing and reciting competitions. Many of the other buildings of the garden were used for literary occasions, feasts and official entertaining.

While in the garden, it is impossible to overlook the pebble mosaics on either side of the paths and the water-sculpted rocks set on plinths. A Chinese garden is less horticulturally oriented than a western garden and its design is much more bound up with its architecture and ornaments than with flower beds and shrubs. However, the Chinese were keen cultivators of 'cult' flowers and plants such as chrysanthemums, peonies and bamboo: all popular subjects for poetic and artistic compositions. The painted woodwork panels and ceiling panels of their buildings echo the Chinese love of these plants and in garden architecture particularly flower and landscape paintings on the woodwork are commonly found.

(Above) The Pavilion of Imperial View in the Imperial Garden is set above a rockery of water-eroded stones. *(Below)* A pebble mosaic in the walkway of the Imperial Garden.

Outside the Forbidden City, and to its south-east, lies the complex of the Imperial Ancestral Temples. It was laid out in the original city plan of the Yong Le emperor, in the 15th century, according to the classical prescriptions of the Zhou dynasty. Zhou ritual texts specified that the ruler, in establishing his capital, should place the ancestral altars to the south-east of his palace and an altar to the soil and grains to the south-west. The founding emperor of the Ming dynasty, the Hong Wu emperor, had arranged his capital in Nanjing according to classical doctrines; after him the Yong Le emperor was equally faithful in creating his new capital.

The temples have been converted into a Workers' Palace and can be visited from the south, through a gate just east of the Gate of Heavenly Peace, or through a gate to the east side

THE IMPERIAL ANCESTRAL TEMPLES — *TAI MIAO*

(Opposite) The Thousand Autumns Pavilion of the Imperial Garden, the Forbidden City.

Plan of Forbidden City
area including
Prospect Hill, Gate of
Heavenly Peace,
Imperial Archives etc.
1. Gate of Heavenly
Peace, *Tian An Men*;
2. Gate of Correct
Deportment, *Duan
Men*;
3. Meridian Gate,
Wu Men;
4. Imperial Ancestral
Temple, *Tai Miao*;
5. Altar to the Soil
and Grains, *She Ji
Tan*;
6. Imperial Archives,
Huang Shi Cheng;
7. Prospect Hill, *Jing
Shan*;
8. Ten Thousand
Springs Pavilion, *Wan
Chun Ting*.

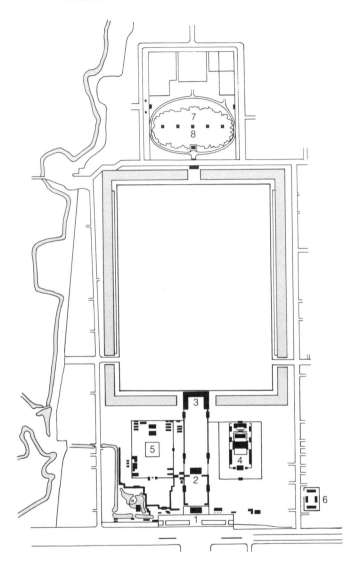

of the approach to the Meridian Gate. If you approach the temples from the south, you cross a stream and pass through a series of gates before entering the central walled compound of the three main halls. The halls are set on a three-tiered white stone terrace with dragon and phoenix motifs on the stonework. The buildings we see today date from the Qing dynasty but were modelled on those of the Ming.

The temples did not always have the present layout. In the **Jia Jing** reign (1522–66) of the Ming dynasty, the emperor was persuaded to build nine separate temples so as to conform more closely with Zhou ritual texts. In 1535, the temples were completed, but only six years later eight out of the nine were burnt down during a severe thunderstorm. The emperor probably took this as a sign of displeasure on the part of Heaven for overspending, and the complex was rebuilt in the simpler form of three main halls.

The **Front Hall**, *Qian Dian*, has been left untouched by the municipal authorities and stands as a grand building, nine bays wide, with painted woodwork panels of dragons and geometrical flower designs. There is little remarkable about this building, for it has the standard double-eaved hip roof, the maximum number of eleven roof guardian figures (only the Hall of Supreme Harmony has one more figure, making twelve) and the standard latticework of hexagonal circle patterns. However, all these design and decorative features indicate the formal importance of the building. It was the place where all the large-scale ceremonies of ancestor worship took place. In the **Middle Hall**, *Zhong Dian*, the Qing imperial family kept the ancestral tablets of all the emperors. The **Rear Hall**, *Hou Dian*, was where the ancestral tablets of remote ancestors were kept. Today, the Middle and Rear Halls are used as recreation centres for workers and have been divided into two floors, partitioned into rooms, given false ceilings and ugly electric light chandeliers. Only the Front Hall has retained its open one-storey interior.

This altar complex was also part of the Yong Le emperor's grand design for his capital, and was completed in 1421. It stands opposite the Imperial Ancestral Temples on the southwest of the Forbidden City. It is entered from the south through a gate just to the west of the Gate of Heavenly Peace, or from the east, through a gate on the west side of the courtyard in front of the Meridian Gate. The altar and its buildings are now a public park, *Zhong Shan Gong Yuan*, named after the Cantonese-born founder of the Chinese republic, Dr Sun Yat Sen, (his name Yat Sen in the northern dialect is phoneticized as Zhong Shan).

THE ALTAR TO THE SOIL AND THE GRAINS — *SHE JI TAN*

The presence of an altar to the soil and grains was important enough to be considered one of the 'prescribed' elements of a capital. Sacrifices to the soil and grains date back to the Bronze Age in China and remained an important feature of imperial worship in an agrarian society. The cosmological significance of this altar is manifested in the overt symbolism of its construction. The altar itself is a large square open to the sky. The square shape represents earth and is thus appropriate for sacrifices to the soil and grains. On the altar are four triangular segments of different coloured earths corresponding to the compass points: white on the west side; black on the north; green on the east; and red to the south. Yellow earth lies at the centre. In imperial times, the soils would have been brought from all parts of the empire. The low boundary wall of the altar has tiles of different colours which also correspond with the compass points.

Twice a year — in the spring planting season and at harvest time — the emperor came in person to the Altar to the Soil and the Grains to offer incense to the spirits. North of the open-air altar is a fine rectangular hall called the **Hall of Prayer**, *Bai Dien*. This building has retained its original Ming roof structure with a deep gable and shallow hip. It was here that preparatory prayers were read before sacrifices. The building to the north of this hall was used as a storehouse for the sacrificial instruments of the altar.

THE IMPERIAL
ARCHIVES —
*HUANG SHI
CHENG*

Within the old Imperial City area on the east side of the Forbidden City stand the Imperial Archives. They are entered through a gate on the east side of the southern end of the road called *Nan Chi Zi*. Although they are on the site of the Ming imperial archives, they have been restored extensively in the Qing dynasty and in recent years.

The buildings of the Imperial Archives are good examples of Chinese stonemasonry. The roofs are set over the stone work in the same manner as those of timber-frame buildings, but the halls have no timber columns; instead the interior is built from stone arches and brick walls, in order to protect the archives against the danger of fire. The buildings contained the written notes of the emperors' daily activities, *Shi Lu*, and imperial edicts. The documents were stored in wood and metal chests

set on stone platforms — another safeguard against fire. The stone walls have small vents to help the circulation of air within the vaults. The vents are fashioned in the shape of cash symbols — one of the eight precious objects used in Chinese decoration.

The Main Hall of the Imperial Archives, the Imperial City.

PROSPECT HILL — *JING SHAN*

Prospect Hill, *Jing Shan*, lies behind the Forbidden City outside its northern gate. It is now a public park, separated from the back of the Forbidden City by a busy main thoroughfare — in imperial times, there was no road to the south of the hill, just a large open space. The hill itself has both practical and geomantic significance. In imperial times, it was used as an orchard, a bird sanctuary and garden for the emperor and his retinue. It also acted as a screen against the northern edge of the palace, shielding the palace buildings from northerly winds and the unpleasant spirits believed to emanate from the north.

The hill was built with the earth excavated from the moats during the initial phase of palace building in the early 15th century. In the Ming dynasty, it was known as the Ten Thousand Years Hill, *Wan Shou Shan*; in the Qing dynasty, it came to be known as Hundred Fruits Hill, *Bai Guo Shan*, because of the orchard planted on its slopes. The names it is known by today are Prospect Hill, *Jing Shan*, and Coal Hill, *Mei Shan*, because some legends have it that coal was buried beneath the hill. The hill is famous in Chinese history as the place where the last Ming emperor, Chong Zhen, hanged himself in despair when rebel troops attacked his city in 1644.

The **five pavilions** on the five low peaks of the hill were built during the Qian Long reign of the Qing dynasty. The pavilions can be seen from within the gardens of the Forbidden City and become 'borrowed' scenery in the palace garden views. The pavilions have a pleasing symmetry which is tempered by their different heights, shapes and roof styles. The two outer pavilions are circular with double eaves. The inner pair are hexagonal with double eaves, and the central pavilion, the **Ten Thousand Springs Pavilion**, *Wan Chun Ting*, is square with triple eaves. All the pavilions are open-framed with no walls, and each once housed the bronze statue of a deity.

BEIHAI

On the western perimeter of the Imperial City lie three interconnected lakes: South Sea, *Nanhai*, Middle Sea, *Zhonghai*, and North Sea, *Beihai*. Of the three, only the northern lake and its halls and pavilions are open to visitors as a public park. The buildings around the other two lakes, collectively known as *Zhongnanhai*, now serve as the residential headquarters of the leaders of the Chinese Communist Party. Visitors who had a chance to see the two southern lakes before 1949, when the Communists came to power, left vivid accounts of beautiful lakeside architecture and an island retreat on the southern lake, where in 1898 the **Empress Dowager** (1835–1908) imprisoned her nephew, the youthful **Guang Xu** emperor (reigned 1875–1908), for trying to institute political reform.

All three lakes have the same source, a river which rises as a spring in the hills to the north-west of the city. A lake was first excavated here more than 800 years ago in the Jin dynasty, when Peking served as a regional capital for the northern Tartars. The Yuan dynasty emperor, Kubilai Khan, also used

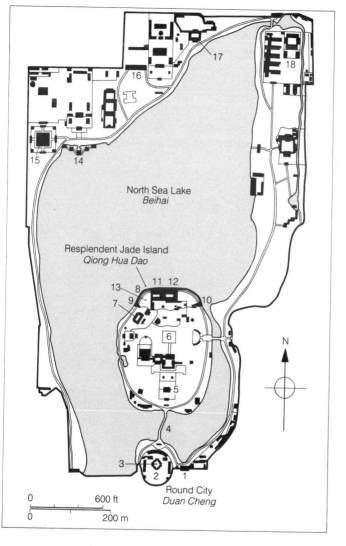

Plan of *Beihai*
1. South Gate, *Nan Men*;
2. Round City, *Duan Cheng*;
3. Receiving Light Hall, *Cheng Guan Dian*;
4. Bridge of Eternal Peace, *Yong An Qiao*;
5. Temple of Eternal Peace, *Yong An Si*;
6. White Dagoba, *Bai Ta*;
7. Chamber for Reading Classics, *Yue Gu Lou*;
8. Floating Gallery, *Yu Lang*;
9. Pavilion of Pleasing Coolness, *Fen Liang Ge*;
10. Tower at the Edge of Clear Waters, *Yi Qing Lou*;
11. Pavilion of the Distant Sails, *Yuan Fan Ge*;
12. Tower of Blue Reflection, *Bi Zhao Lou*;
13. Gathering Dew Dish, *Cheng Lu Pan*;
14. Five Dragon Pavilions, *Wu Long Ting*;
15. Temple of Pure Land, *Ji Le Shi Jie*;
16. Nine Dragon Screen, *Jiu Long Bi*;
17. Lodge of the Quiet Heart, *Jing Xin Zhai*;
18. Altar of Silkworms, *Can Tan*.

this lake area as a palace resort, and the Venetian merchant-traveller Marco Polo was received here at lakeside palaces in the late 13th century.

However, it was in the Ming dynasty, when the Yong Le emperor was rebuilding Peking in the early 15th century, that the lake was re-excavated and made into three distinct basins.

The wooden ceremonial archway, or *pai lou*, marking the northern end of the Bridge of Eternal Peace, *Beihai*.

The lakes as we see them in their present form date from those 15th-century renovations.

During the Ming period the lakes were known collectively as Golden Sea, *Jin Hai*, and the palaces and pavilions around the lakes were called Western Park, *Xi Yuan*. Sadly, none of the original Ming architecture of the Xi Yuan has survived. Most of the buildings of the lake palaces date from either the 18th or 19th centuries and were landscaped by the Qian Long emperor and the Empress Dowager. The names we know the lakes by today date from the Kang Xi era of the 17th century.

Most visitors to *Beihai* enter through the south gate, which lies just to the north-west of the rear gate of the Forbidden City. However, the park does have two other gates, to the east and to the north.

The lake is the centre of the composition of the imperial pleasure park. At its south-eastern corner is an island, **Resplendent Jade Island**, *Qiong Hua Dao*, which is also sometimes called Hortensia Island. The island is an artificial mound, created from the earth excavated when the lake was being dug. On the summit of the mound is a striking plain white dagoba, an Indian-style Buddhist pagoda, which is the landmark of the park. It is an appropriate emblem for the park, which encompasses a curious mixture of religious buildings, storehouses for cultural relics and garden architecture.

Most of the buildings of *Beihai* actually lie either on the island of Resplendent Jade or on the northern and eastern shoreline. The lake itself takes up well over half of the 68ha (170 acres) of the park and is famous as a venue for skating in winter. Ice-skating is an old custom in China, and the Qing emperors were fond of organizing ice displays which involved feats of martial prowess. The Qian Long emperor came here in winter to watch hundreds of skaters perform complicated displays such as shooting at moving targets while skating at full speed. In summer, the waters of the lake have a bright fringe of pink and green when the lotuses come into flower. Boat expeditions, which could cover the length of all three lakes, were often organized by the emperor for the enjoyment of his palace women and retinue.

Today, the park authorities have introduced fibreglass gimmick boats, funfairs, a children's amusement area and a plethora of tourist shops which look wholly out of place next to the willows, red-columned galleries and pavilions that line the shore. For the local people, they are badly needed centres for recreation, but it means that a great feat of the imagination is required to envisage how this park must have looked a century ago when planted, tended and decorated as an imperial resort. Many buildings in the park are derelict, some have been converted to modern usage with no understanding of original function or decoration, and others are currently being restored. Garden maintenance in *Beihai* is poor.

A notable feature of the park is **Round City**, *Duan Cheng*, a fortified circular enclosure which lies just to the west of the South Gate. It stands separated from the main park by a 5m (16ft) high crenellated wall. Inside the raised enclosure is a central Buddha hall surrounded by ancient junipers, small pavilions and a grand rockery. This hall, the **Receiving Light Hall**, *Cheng Guang Dian*, has the same ground plan as that of the corner towers of the Forbidden City, namely a stepped square cross. However, unlike the four corner towers, the hall has only two sets of eaves, with the upper roof a single hip-and-gable form. The roof has yellow tiles with green ridge and eaves ends. Throughout the park, you will see many of these two-coloured roofs, either green with yellow, or like this hall, yellow with green.

There has been a temple hall on this site since the Ming dynasty (earlier dynasties had palaces here), but the present building dates from a restoration in 1890 under the patronage of the Empress Dowager. Most of the decorative design work is in the classical imperial *he xi* style, a feature of temple buildings founded under imperial patronage, with the traditional whirling flower patterns set on either side of dragon panels. However, the ceiling panels have a less common motif of four cranes set around the central circle of double dragons. The Buddha image in the hall is often referred to as a jade Buddha, but the stone itself is not a true jade; it dates from the early 18th century.

In a small, tiled, open pavilion in front of the Receiving Light Hall, is one of the most valuable treasures of the park — an olive-black jade bowl carved with sinuous dragons and strange sea creatures in a foaming sea. The bowl dates from the Yuan dynasty; it was a gift to Kubilai Khan and was stored in a building in his palace on this site. Standing at 0.66m (2 ft)

The Receiving Light Hall in the Round City, *Beihai.*

high and 1.5m (5 ft) across, it is a marvellous piece of work and serves very well as a piece of open-air sculpture. Carved from a single piece of jade, its shape is an imperfect circle.

You can leave the Round City to the north by a flight of steps which leads directly down to the **Bridge of Eternal Peace,** *Yong An Qiao*, leading to Resplendent Jade Island. At each end of the bridge stand a matching pair of decorative arches known in Chinese as *pai lou*. These arches are believed, like pagodas, to have derived from Indian Buddhist architectural forms. The *pai lou* is thought to have derived from the Indian *torana* or ceremonial arch. They serve no practical function except to give an entrance, roadway or bridge a certain ceremonial splendour.

The jade bowl of Kubilai Khan in the Round City, *Beihai.*

The island is dense with many remarkable and charming buildings. The white **dagoba** was built in 1651 in honour of the visit of the Tibetan spiritual leader, the Fifth Dalai Lama, to the court of the first Qing emperor Shun Zhi. The Sanskrit inscription on the alcove on the south side of the dagoba reads, 'Door of the Light of the Eye'. The **Temple of Eternal Peace**, *Yong An Si*, which stretches out beneath the dagoba on the south-facing slope of the island, was also built to mark the same occasion.

The halls and pavilions of the Temple of Eternal Peace dominate the south slope of the island, but the northern and eastern slopes have a large number of decorative buildings set on rocks, which give good views across the trees and lake, but some are hidden behind a wall to create a glade of cool tranquillity. However, the large number of visitors to the park today ensures that there is little tranquillity anywhere. Nonetheless, there are some interesting (and precipitous!) walks around the rockeries on the northeastern slope of the island with paths cut through grottoes, that lead up to pavilions and down into small decorative entrances. My recommendation is to walk down to the Chamber for Reading the Classics, and stroll round the northeastern shore of the island to the jetty on the northern tip.

The **Chamber for Reading the Classics**, *Yue Gu Lou*, is my favourite building on the island. Built in the shape of a half-moon it has two storeys, the upper one of which is a gallery which is open on one side so as to overlook the inner courtyard. The building was commissioned by the Qian Long emperor in the 18th century to house a fine collection of antique calligraphy inscriptions on stone tablets. The collection is open to view and is displayed in a series of cases laid out around the gallery walkway.

From the Chamber for Reading the Classics you can walk northwards to the grand, double-tiered covered walkway that skirts the entire northern shore of the island. The walkway, known as the **Floating Gallery**, *Yu Lang*, ends and begins with a square single-eaved pavilion set above a high, square masonry terrace. The pavilion on the north-western shore is called the **Pavilion of Pleasing Coolness**, *Fen Liang Ge*, and that of the north-eastern shore is the **Tower at the Edge of Clear Waters**, *Yi Qing Lou*. The double tier of the Floating Gallery interlocks with two double-storeyed halls on the northern shore, the **Pavilion of the Distant Sails**, *Yuan Fan Ge*, and the **Tower of Blue Reflection**, *Bi Zhao Lou*. Where the gallery joins the halls, the top walkway slopes upward to meet the upper floors of the halls. The Tower of Blue Reflection now houses part of the famous Fang Shan Restaurant, where recipes from the Qing court kitchens are served up in an opulently ugly setting.

A pleasant and cooling way to gain a view of the north slopes of Resplendent Jade Island is to take a boat from the jetty opposite the Fang Shan Restaurant to the northern shore of the lake. Look up and you will see the picturesque white dagoba dominating the wooded slopes of the island like an enormous exotic white bottle.

Another landmark on the north-eastern slopes of the island is a bronze statue displayed on top of a tall white stone column carved with dragons. The statue is of a man holding up a dish above his head. The dish is to catch the night dew and the statue is called the **Gathering Dew Dish**, *Cheng Lu Pan*. The statue was put up in the Qian Long era and is said to represent someone who was sent to collect the dew for the Han dynasty Wu Di emperor. **Han Wu Di** (reigned 140–87 BC) was a keen practitioner of Daoist occult alchemy and hoped that he could discover the elixir of life. Daoist recipes for the pursuit of immortality demanded such esoteric practices as chewing rock minerals, swallowing ground pearls and drinking dew!

When you arrive on the northern shore of the lake you will see five symmetrical pavilions built on a stone terrace over the water. Such clusters of buildings were very popular in Chinese garden architecture where the idea was to create a focus of architectural interest in a place of natural beauty. The five pavilions are known as the **Five Dragon Pavilions**, *Wu Long Ting*; the dragon motif is created by the zig-zag shape of the paths between the pavilions, the shape being said to resemble that of a dragon's back. All the pavilions are square in form, but diversity is created by the varied roof heights and shapes: the two outer pavilions are the lowest and have one layer of eaves; the two inner pavilions have double square eaves; and the central, and largest, pavilion has a lower set of square eaves crowned with a circular upper roof. The roofs have green glazed tiles with decorative yellow edges and ridges. The pavilions are linked by a series of bridges built in white stone. The baluster caps of these bridge walkways are in the form of a pomegranate, a shape favoured in the decorative balusters of garden architecture.

One of the most impressive pieces of architecture in *Beihai* is the Buddhist **Temple of Pure Land**, *Ji Le Shi Jie*, in the north-west corner of the park. Built in 1770, during the Qian Long reign, it was and remains the largest square wooden structure in China with a floor space of 1,200m² (12,900ft²). The great weight of the double-eaved plain square roof is supported by a series of massive interior columns. The hall should contain an image of the Guan Yin bodhisattva, popularly known as the Goddess of Mercy, but the building is currently being restored and the interior is empty. Like all Buddhist temples being restored, it may be difficult to find out whether the Buddhist image placed in the hall after renovation is the original one prior to closure. Owing to the widespread destruction of cultural relics during the so-called Cultural Revolution in the 1960s, many newly restored temples have either been allocated recently carved images copied from photographs of lost originals, or have been given images from other temples now destroyed. Throughout China, few temples remain and those that do have lost most of their religious treasures.

Also on the northern shore area of the lake is a **Nine Dragon Screen**, *Jiu Long Bi*, built in 1756. The screen thus dates from the same period as the Nine Dragon Screen in the Forbidden City, the reign of the Qian Long emperor. The nine dragons in this screen are also set in wave-filled seas separated by sculpted

(Above) The Nine Dragon Screen, *Beihai*.

(Below) A detail from the Nine Dragon Screen, *Beihai*.

mountains, but the postures and their bold lively appearance differs from those of the Forbidden City. The screen at *Beihai*, (25.86m (85 ft) long and 6.65m (22 ft) high), is not as long as the one in the Forbidden City, but is higher.

At the rear of the park is an enclosed garden which is a separate world from the open vistas and vast expanses of *Beihai*. The garden is the **Lodge of the Quiet Heart**, *Jing Xin Zhai*. The garden as we see it today, features design details from the late 19th century and from recent renovations. At the turn of the century, this garden was a favoured retreat of the Empress Dowager who ruled China first through her son, the **Tong Zhi** emperor (reigned 1862–74) and then through her nephew, the Guang Xu emperor. She even had a hand in picking the child emperor **Pu Yi** (reigned 1909–12), who was to be China's last emperor. She was an extravagant and uncultured patron of architecture and most of the buildings that she favoured with lavish rebuilding usually suffered from a surfeit of decoration.

A secret world is created in this garden, with small halls and pavilions set around a winding pool framed by a massive rockery. The garden has a stiffness and formality that sets it apart from the plainer, subtler and more pleasing gardens of Jiangsu and Zhejiang provinces. At present, parts of the garden are very shabby and some sections serve as the living quarters for the park staff. But the closely spaced buildings and winding paths do give an excellent idea of the detailed art of garden building in China. There is a covered walkway which climbs round the back of the garden and looks out over the different areas of the pond and rockery. The garden buildings all have plain rustic roofs of unglazed tiles, red painted columns and interior beamwork featuring Suzhou-style paintings of landscapes or scenes of birds, animals and flowers.

There is much else in *Beihai* not described in these pages. For example, on the eastern shore is the site of the **Altar of Silkworms**, *Can Tan*, where the empress and her attendants ceremonially tended mulberry bushes (silkworm larvae feed only on mulberry leaves) and spun the thread. This was the *yin* or female equivalent of the emperor's formal ploughing ceremony at the Temple of Agriculture. The park has its quiet moments in the early mornings before office hours, when the visitors are mainly old folk out to take the air and work on their callisthenic exercise routines. However, as lovely as the park is in the early morning hours, very few of the buildings themselves are open to visitors. The best advice is to start early with a walk around the lake and stay long enough to wait for the halls and temples to open. Most public parks in China open at dawn and special monuments can be visited from either 9 a.m. or 10 a.m. until 4 p.m.

THE TEMPLE OF HEAVEN — *Tian Tan*

The history of the Temple of Heaven is an interesting chapter in the evolution of imperial sacrificial ceremonies. When the Yong Le emperor built an altar here for the worship of Heaven, he was keeping up an antique tradition of sacrifices and ceremonies that marked the solstices. In the Zhou-dynasty text, the 'Record of Rites', *Li Ji*, (see page 8), there is a passage which refers to the ordering of the cosmos through offerings to Heaven:

> When thus at the felicitous place (namely, the site chosen for the capital) they (the rulers) presented their offerings to the gods in the

suburbs and made announcements to Heaven . . . the winds and rain were duly regulated, and the cold and heat came each in its proper time, so that the sage ruler had only to stand with his face to the south, and order prevailed under Heaven.

However, the Zhou texts were not uniform in their descriptions of rituals or the way in which various elements such as Heaven, Earth, the gods and the spirits were worshipped. This inconsistency led to a number of scholarly debates in the Ming dynasty on whether Heaven and Earth should be worshipped together at one altar or separately at two different locations. The debate was finally, but not conclusively, settled in the Jia Jing reign of the Ming dynasty, with the building of a separate altar in the northern suburbs for the worship of the Earth and its associated spirits of the mountains and rivers.

Yet as much as Ming emperors debated the authenticity of and precedent for their sacrifices, they maintained a totally new tradition initiated by the founding Ming emperor Hong

Temple of Heaven
Complex Plan
1. West Gate;
2. South Gate;
3. Altar of Heaven, *Huan Qiu*;
4. Imperial Vault of Heaven, *Huang Qiong Yu*;
5. Red Stairway Bridge, *Dan Bi Qiao*;
6. Hall for Good Harvests, *Qi Nian Dian*;
7. Long Walkway, *Chang Lang*;
8. Animal Slaughter Hall, *Zai Xing Ting*;
8a. Ceremonial kitchen and store, *Shen Chu Shen*;
9. Double Circle Pavilion, *Shuang Huan Ting*;
10. Fasting Palace, *Zhai Gong*;
11. Original outer wall of Temple of Heaven (now demolished).

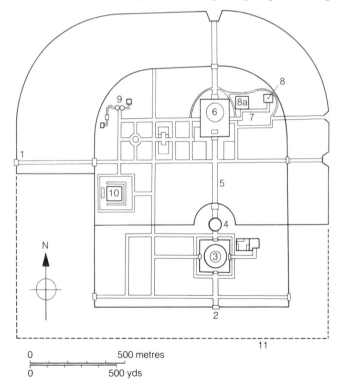

Wu. Until his time, all sacrifices to Heaven had been made at an open air site. However, the Hong Wu emperor, at his Altar of Heaven in Nanjing, built a ceremonial hall inside which the major sacrifice to Heaven took place. This was a wholly new departure in the history of imperial sacrifices to Heaven and most of the succeeding Ming emperors followed the formula set by the founding emperor. But by the late Ming period and throughout the Qing dynasty, the major sacrifice to Heaven reverted to its open-air location.

The whole complex of the Temple of Heaven, or Altar of Heaven, is a vast walled enclosure of 273ha (682 acres) which lies to the east of the central north–south axis of the capital in the southern suburbs. You can enter the Temple of Heaven park from one of its four gates on the cardinal points. Most tourist buses deposit their passengers at the western gate, but I prefer to enter by the southern gate as it involves a walk all the way along the central axis of the complex, the major part of which is an enormous raised ceremonial pavement known as the **Red Stairway Bridge**, *Dan Bi Qiao*. The walk gives a clear impression of the grand scale and harmonious composition of the architecture.

The altar complex dates from the Yong Le era of the Ming dynasty; halls and an altar were first built in 1420. The layout we see today dates from the 16th-century Jia Jing reign but the buildings themselves are all Qing structures. The great enclosure is circular in the north and square in the south, to represent Heaven (the circle) and Earth (the square). Within the original main wall is another smaller and identically shaped wall creating an enclosure which contains the most important ceremonial buildings and the altar itself.

All the major ceremonial buildings and the altar are aligned along a north–south axis with the altar in the south. At the centre is the Imperial Vault of Heaven, which is linked by the Red Stairway Bridge to the Hall for Good Harvests in the north. This blue-roofed, triple-eaved circular hall, which is the landmark of the Temple of Heaven, has almost become the symbol of the Chinese tourist industry; it is used as an emblem on anything from keyrings to bottles of beer! The Hall for Good Harvests is probably the single most famous building in China and, unsurprisingly, many people think that the building is the Temple of Heaven.

The Temple of Heaven complex is now a public park (it was a public execution ground in the 1930s), and has all the paraphernalia of public parks anywhere in China — gaudy amusement areas, cafes, shops and photo booths. The sacred tranquillity of halls, terraces and ancient junipers and cypresses has given way to the hurly-burly of flag- and megaphone-led tourist groups.

The **Altar of Heaven**, *Huan Qiu*, stands as a circle within a square enclosure of low, red walls roofed with blue tiles. There are four entrances into the enclosure set on the compass points. Each entrance is a triple gate in white stone sculpted with decorative cloud patterns on the 'wings' above the lintels and on panels at the base of each column. The structure of the altar dates from 1530, the Jia Jing reign period. In this period the altar was built in blue stones. Further alterations were undertaken in 1749 in the reign of the Qing dynasty Qian Long emperor, who had the altar enlarged and the original blue stones replaced with white ones.

The Altar of Heaven approached through a series of ceremonial stone archways, Temple of Heaven.

The altar is an impressive structure, composed of three tiers of white stone, inset with four flights of triple-layered steps, to the north, east, south and west. Strict axiality and numerical symbolism are significant features of the altar, which was built as a symbol of Heaven. All its measurements and elements are in odd numbers, which are *yang*, and correspond with Heaven (even numbers are *yin* and correspond with Earth). The highest level of the altar is 9 *chang* in diameter (a *chang* is a unit of measure which was equivalent to 0.32 of a metre in the Ming period and 0.31 of a metre in the Qing dynasty until 1840); the second level is 15 *chang* across; and the third level has a diameter of 21 *chang*. The stones of the surfaces of the terraces are laid out in multiples of 9 (the number representing Heaven). The surface of the upper terrace has a central stone surrounded by 9 concentric rings, the innermost of which has 9 stones and the outermost of which has 81 (9 × 9). On the middle and lower terraces, the concentric bands of stones likewise increase in multiples of 9 down to the outermost ring of the lowest layer which has 243 stones (9 × 27). Even the number of stone baluster caps of the walls around the terraces are in multiples of 9.

On the day of the winter solstice, the day when *yin*, the force of the earth, was waning and *yang* forces returned to ascendancy, the emperor climbed the altar and made a sacrificial offering of an ox, sheep and a pig, as well as a libation of wine, in front of the spirit tablets (small wooden boards inscribed with the name of the spirit) of Heaven, the supreme god Shang Di (a deity first recorded in the Shang dynasty, 1480–1050 BC), the moon, sun, clouds, rain, wind, thunder and 28 constellations. Set out on the altar were pennants and awnings. Court officials stood around the terraces of the altar according to rank. Sacred music was played during these ceremonies on chimes, gongs and drums. The musical instruments used in the ceremonies are now on display in the front hall of the Fasting Palace. In addition to the winter solstice sacrifice, emperors came here in the event of natural disasters, such as flood or drought, to pray to Heaven for the return of order and clement, seasonal weather.

To the north of the altar stands the **Imperial Vault of Heaven**, *Huang Qiong Yu*, in a circular walled enclosure. It was here that the spirit tablets of Heaven and tablets for the imperial ancestors were stored, on stone platforms. The Imperial Vault of Heaven is a round, wooden hall with a single conical roof of blue tiles. The roof originally had green tiles, but the colour was changed to blue when the building was renovated in 1753 during the Qian Long era. The building stands on a single white stone terrace. There is an imperial carriageway, a carved stone ramp, at the centre of the steps leading up to the terrace from the south.

The Imperial Vault of Heaven, the Temple of Heaven.

The remarkable feature of this enclosure is the acoustic quality of the perfectly circular wall that surrounds the Imperial Vault of Heaven. The wall, 6m (19ft) high, is sometimes called 'Echo Wall', because a whispered sound made on one side of it is audible on the other. Another acoustic phenomenon in this enclosure is the Triple Sounding Stone, a stone slab which lies to the south of the hall. If you stand on the stone and clap, the stone will resonate giving back a triple echo. I have never been able to experience either of these echo effects because of the number of people clapping and whispering simultaneously. Perhaps if one came very early, it might be possible to try them out.

You have to leave the enclosure of the Imperial Vault of Heaven from the south gate because there is no north gate, and then walk round the wall to join up with the **Red Staircase**

The Hall for Good Harvests, the main building of the Temple of Heaven.

Bridge (or walkway), *Dan Bi Qiao*, that leads to the **Hall for Good Harvests**, *Qi Nian Dian*, in the north. The hall is the main building of the complex and is as rich in symbolism as the altar to the south. The tiles on the triple eaves (triple because three is a *yang* numer) are blue and said to represent the sky. Before the Qian Long period, the tiles on the three eaves were blue, yellow and green. However, when the Qian Long emperor had the building renovated, the roof was given a single tile colour and the hall was renamed with the title it bears today.

The hall sits on three terraces with three separate imperial carriageways (see page 57) at the centre of the southern flight of steps. The lower ramp is carved with a small band of waves out of which rise three mountains topped with clouds. The second ramp depicts two phoenixes, the *yin* symbol of the empress. The uppermost ramp shows two dragons amidst the clouds. The baluster caps on the walls of the three layers of terraces also echo the three themes of the imperial carriage-way: the baluster caps of the lower level of the terrace have cloud carvings; the second level caps have phoenix motifs and the upper level baluster caps are carved with dragons. The gilded decorative work on the beamwork of this hall likewise features the imperial dragon-and-phoenix motif.

The interior of the Hall for Good Harvest seldom fails to impress visitors. It is a single open space with a central 'lantern ceiling' (see page 36). The lowest roof layer rests on the wooden framework supported by the 12 outer pillars enclosed by the wall of the building. The weight of the second layer of roof is carried by the circle of 12 inner pillars in the interior of the hall. The third layer of the roof is carried by the four central pillars and the crossbeams supported by every fourth column of the 12 inner pillars. Each of the inner support columns is a massive piece of timber, some of which came from the forests of Yunnan in south-west China and some of which came from the United States of America during the rebuilding of the hall between 1890 and 1896. The four central support columns, a towering 19m (62ft) high and covered with a beautiful goldleaf design of flowers and leaves, represent the four seasons. The inner ring of 12 columns symbolizes the months of the year and the total 28 pillars supporting the roof represent the 28 constellations worshipped during the sacrifices to Heaven.

The subsidiary spirits were worshipped in the side halls to the north, east and west of the Hall for Good Harvests. These halls are now used as display areas and shops.

A covered 72-bay Long Walkway leads out from the eastern door of the enclosure around the Hall for Good Harvest to a complex of halls, where the sacrificial animals were slaughtered and prepared. The halls are in a bad state of repair and currently not open to the public. The Long Walkway is not in good decorative order either, but is a wonderful place to enjoy park life — old men playing dominoes and students reading in the shade.

To the west of the Hall for Good Harvests is a **Double Circle Pavilion**, *Shuang Huan Ting*, which is a modern addition and an excellent example of whimsical park architecture. The pavilion has a roof of two interlocked circles in blue tiles with yellow edging.

To the south of the Double Circle Pavilion is the **Fasting Palace**, *Zhai Gong*, where the emperor spent the night before the winter solstice sacrifice. In fact, the emperor had to fast for three days before the sacrifice to Heaven, but the first two days of abstinence were spent within the Forbidden City and only the third day was spent in the Fasting Palace. The palace is surrounded by a moat (dry at present) with an exterior covered walkway overlooking the moat. The walkway, in contrast to the formal decoration found elsewhere on the buildings of this complex, has charming *Su shi*-style paintings of landscapes, birds and flowers.

Inside the front hall of the Fasting Palace (called a 'beamless hall' because it has no timber columns and instead has brickwork vaults), there is a display of the ceremonial objects and instruments used in the sacrifices to Heaven. At the back of the enclosure, you can look into the private chambers of the emperor, which have been renovated.

The Altar of Earth.

THE ALTAR OF EARTH — *Di Tan*

The Altar of Earth, the second most important of the surviving suburban altars of Peking, lies in the northern suburbs of the city, just outside the old city walls, north-east of the Everlasting Stability Gate. It is now a public park and fewer of its buildings have survived and been renovated than in the Temple of Heaven park. The Fasting Palace of this altar has been turned into a recreation centre, and other buildings serve as restaurants and tourist souvenir shops.

The Altar of Earth was first built in 1530 during the Ming dynasty Jia Jing reign, after a debate on the worship of Heaven and Earth made the emperor decide that the two should be worshipped separately at two different sites. The original name for this altar was the Square and Watery Altar, *Fang Ze Tan*. Since earliest times in China the square has been a symbol of the earth, and the element associated with Earth is moisture, because the earth is *yin* and of the female principle. The altar complex was renovated under the patronage of the Qing dynasty emperors Yong Zheng (reigned 1723–35) and Qian Long.

The deity of the Earth was worshipped at the summer solstice when *yin* forces were in the ascendant with the shortening of the days. Also worshipped with the Earth in the same ceremonies were the spirits of the Four Rivers, Four Seas, Five Mountains and Five Peaks. The long, rectangular carved stone platforms on which their spirit tablets were placed can still be seen set out around the top level of the Altar.

The corresponding colour of the Earth is yellow, so yellow is used in the tiling around the complex. The altar itself is a two-tiered square terrace within a square walled enclosure. All the numbers used in the measurements and elements of the altar are even, *yin*, numbers, just as at the Altar of Heaven all the numbers used in measurements are uneven and *yang*. The Altar of Earth, like the Altar of Heaven, was built as a cosmic symbol.

Thus the altar has 2 layers, 4 sets of steps, each of which has 8 steps, and stone slabs set out in circuits enlarging by 8 from the centre. The central circuit of stones on the top terrace is 36 and all subsequent circuits increase by an additional 8 stones until you reach the outer circuit of the lower layer of the altar which has 156 stones. We also know that the dimensions of the original Ming altar on the site were in even or *yin* number multiples.

Like the Temple of Heaven complex, the Altar of Earth contained a building in which the original spirit tablets were kept. This was the **Imperial Veneration Chamber**, *Huang Zhi Shi*, to the south of the altar. This chamber is the Cultural Relics of the Altar of Earth Exhibition Hall, and is currently not open to visitors.

As an interesting footnote, you will not see any sacrificial furnaces around the Altar of Earth as there are around the Altar of Heaven. This is because the sacrifices to the deity of the Earth were buried rather than burned, as they were to the spirit of Heaven.

THE ALTARS OF THE SUN & MOON —
Ri Tan & Yue Tan
In the late 1520s, the emperor Jia Jing spent much of his time commissioning debates on court ritual and ceremonies. His preoccupation with ritual was to make him one of the great architectural patrons of Peking, because it was he who decided to build the suburban altars of the Earth, Sun, Moon and Agriculture. The Board of Rites, responsible to the emperor for the maintenance of court ritual, persuaded the emperor that as the Tang and Song emperors had had separate altars for the Sun and Moon in the eastern and western suburbs respectively, he too should have such altars. Both altars were completed in 1530. However, none of the original Ming buildings or altar structures survive, as both complexes underwent extensive renovation in the Qing dynasty.

The **Altar of the Sun**, *Ri Tan*, is in the eastern suburbs of the city and lay outside the old city walls. The altar and its buildings have now been incorporated into a public park and most of the old buildings have been turned into shops and a restaurant. However, the altar itself remains as a single-tiered square terrace set within the circle of an enclosure wall. The altar, dedicated to the Sun and therefore embodying the *yang* principle, was built with measurements in odd numbers. The tiles of the altar walls are red, the colour corresponding to the east. The ceremonies for the worship of the sun took place at the spring equinox, a date in the Chinese lunar calendar known as the 'Beginning of Spring' (*Li Chun*). Sun worship was not as important a rite as the worship of Heaven and Earth, and many Ming and Qing emperors did not personally take part in the ceremonies.

The **Altar of the Moon**, *Yue Tan*, in the western suburbs of the city, is also now part of a public park, its ceremonial buildings badly neglected or converted to more practical purposes. But the altar itself, a one-tiered square terrace within a square, walled enclosure, has survived. The altar was built with measurements in even, *yin*, numbers. The corresponding colour of the west is white, and the altar enclosure walls are therefore topped with white glazed tiles. The utensils used during the sacrifice were also white. The sacrifices to the moon took place at the autumn equinox, the 'Beginning of Autumn' (*Li Qiu*) in the Chinese lunar calendar.

The imperial city of Peking was a well-fortified enclosure, as were most Chinese cities in pre-modern times. The **walls** were designed to create a controlled space between city and countryside. In the Ming and Qing periods, Peking had 16 city **gates**: the southern enclosure of the city covering 24.8km^2 (9.3 square miles) known as the Chinese City in the Qing period, had seven gates; the northern section of the capital covering 35km^2 (13 square miles), known as the Tartar City in the Qing dynasty, had nine gates which were arranged so that there were three gates on the eastern, southern and western perimeters and only two on the northern side.

Like the Forbidden City, the city walls were surrounded by a **moat**. The earth excavated to create the moat was used to make the enormous rammed earth cores of the walls which were then encased with bricks. The grey bricks of the walls were laid against the inner core of earth and gravel with a layer of lime. The moat stood 50m (162ft) from the walls and was 30m (97ft) wide. The walls of Tartar City stood 11.5m (37ft) high and were 16m (52ft) broad at the top and 19.5m (63ft) broad at the base. The Tartar City area was of prime strategic importance because it was here that the emperor dwelt. The walls of the Chinese city, a mainly residential area, were smaller and less well fortified.

The city walls were torn down in the 1950s to make way for new express roads round and through the city. The present route of the number 44 bus in Peking follows the perimeter of the old city walls, and on display inside the buses on route 44 are old black and white photographs of the walls, towers and gates of the city.

Two of the original **corner towers** still remain in Peking: one of the two is in the south-east section of the city and can be seen from the window of trains departing from Peking railway station. These towers are massive defensive fortresses in grey brick with a double-eaved roof of green tiles. The outer corners of the top layer of eaves has a small, decorative, gable structure. All the way round the walls of the towers are lines of square windows which would have been used as firing positions. In addition to the corner towers the city walls had terraces and rampart towers at regular intervals to accommodate concentrations of troops in the case of attack.

IMPERIAL
CITY WALLS,
TOWERS &
GATES

The Fore Gate, marking the entrance between the Inner and Outer (Tartar and Chinese) city areas of Peking.

Of the city gates that still remain, none was more important than **Fore Gate**, *Qian Men*, which marked the boundary between the Tartar and Chinese cities. The gate is on the north–south axis line that runs through the centre of the city, and stands directly to the south of the Gate of Heavenly Peace thus, in modern times, marking the southern boundary of *Tian An Men* Square. The walls that once abutted the gate have disappeared and it now stands in grand isolation as a reminder of the majesty of imperial Peking as buses rattle and whir under its eaves. A major defensive structure, the gate has two separate towers, one of wood and one of stone set above masonry platforms. These two gate towers were set above a 'U' shaped walled enclosure which acted as an inner chamber between the two sets of entrance tunnels beneath the gate towers. The northern gate tower is a wooden, decorative structure and the southern tower is a stone archery tower which served to defend the gate. This masonry tower was destroyed by European troops during the Boxer Rebellion in 1900 and was later rebuilt under the supervision of a German architect. Both the inner and outer towers have a central entrance which would, in imperial times, have remained closed to ordinary traffic and been opened only to allow the passage of the emperor on his way to and from sacrifices at the altars in the southern suburbs.

THE DRUM & BELL TOWERS — *Gu Lou & Zhong Lou*

The Drum and Bell Towers, like the Fore Gate, lie on the central north–south axis line of the city, to the north of Prospect Hill in the northern district of Peking. Both towers are now open as public monuments and demand a stiff climb up steep steps. The steps are good practice for the Great Wall!

The **Drum Tower**, *Gu Lou*, lies to the south of the Bell Tower. A Drum Tower was first built near the present location during the Yuan dynasty in 1272. The present location dates from the rebuilding of Peking as a capital by the Yong Le emperor, in 1420. The tower was extensively renovated throughout both the Ming and Qing dynasties, with the last major restoration in imperial times taking place in 1894 during the Guang Xu reign. The tower consists of a masonry platform intersected at ground level by tunnel vaults (the vaults now house a tourist shop), and an upper wooden hall with a double-eaved, hip-and-gable roof in green tiles. Around the first floor of the wooden hall is an open-air gallery which gives an excellent view of the city below. The two horned dragon acroteria, *chi wen*, at either end of the roof ridge, face outwards, warding off any passing evil spirit. Inside the high-ceilinged, open interior of the tower hall are massive buttressed columns which hold up the enormous weight of the roof. There is a collection of drums on display on which the night watches were sounded from dusk to dawn.

The Drum Tower.

The Bell Tower.

The **Bell Tower**, *Zhong Lou*, to the north of the Drum Tower, is a smaller building, a brick hall on a masonry platform. Like the Drum Tower it has a double-eaved, hip-and-gable roof of green tiles with identical horned dragon acroteria. The first Bell Tower was built near the site of this present tower in the Yuan dynasty. The present structure dates from the 18th century during the reign of the Qian Long emperor, who replaced the earlier wooden structure, which had burnt down, with a stone and brick building to make it less vulnerable to fire. The bell was struck at dawn to signal the end of the night watch and was also struck once in the evening to mark the beginning of the night watch.

THE IMPERIAL PARKS

There is a long tradition of imperial parks in Chinese history. We know from historical records that the first emperor of China, **Qin Shi Huang Di** (reigned 221–210 BC), built a magnificent palace and park on his unification of the country in 221 BC. No imperial parks of the pre-Ming period survive in their original form, but some of the parks landscaped by Ming and Qing emperors were built on the ruins of parks of former dynasties. The parks themselves were retreats from the ceremonial formality of the winter palaces and often had small zoos, bird reserves, hunting forests and temples within their perimeters. They were obviously built for the pursuit of pleasure and as a healthy environment in which the emperor, his wives and many children could enjoy the warmer months.

Garden building and the associated pleasures of garden life were taken very seriously and sometimes to the point of obsession, in particular by the **Qian Long** emperor (reigned 1736–95). The Qian Long emperor was the most prolific garden builder in late imperial China despite being conscious of the great expenditure involved. In a memorial inscription erected in the Garden of Perfect Brightness (often called the Old Summer Palace, and now in ruins), he referred to the frugality of his father, the **Yong Zheng** emperor (reigned 1723–35) and grandfather, the **Kang Xi** emperor (reigned 1662–1722) and how they put duty before pleasure. He then went on to justify the expensive art of garden building:

> 'Every emperor and ruler, when he has retired from audience and has finished his public duties, must have a garden where he may stroll and look about and relax his heart. If he has a suitable place to do this, it will refresh his mind and regulate his emotions, but if not he will become engrossed in sensual pleasure and lose his willpower.
> (Translation of inscription from *Summer Palaces of the Ch'ing (Qing) dynasty* by C.B. Malone. Urbana Press 1934.

The emperors of the **Ming** dynasty (1368–1644) spent most

(Opposite) The Long Gallery, the Garden of Ease and Harmony.

of their leisure time in the lakeside palaces of the Western Park within the Imperial City (see p. 80). The three lakes of the Western Park — *Beihai*, *Zhonghai*, and *Nanhai* — also remained popular with the emperors of the **Qing** dynasty (1644–1912). However, the Qing emperors, with their nomadic legacy of extended hunting expeditions, took delight in renovating old gardens and building new ones in the hills to the north-west of the capital and also out beyond the Great Wall at Chengde.

The Kang Xi, Yong Zheng and Qian Long emperors created five major gardens in the north-western district outside the capital. One of these, the Garden of Pure Ripples, *Qing Yi Yuan*, was landscaped around a natural lake which had been an imperial park in the **Jin** dynasty (1125–1235), when it was known as Golden Hill, *Jin Shan*, and then later as Jar Hill, *Weng Shan*. After the Jin, the Ming emperors also had a park built here and called it Beautiful Hills Garden, *Hao Shan Yuan*, because of its excellent view of the Western Hills. During the reign of the Qian Long emperor the park was renovated and given its name the Garden of Pure Ripples. We now know this garden, the only one to have survived of the original five, by its 19th-century name, the Garden of Ease and Harmony, *Yi He Yuan*, but its popular name amongst foreigners is the New Summer Palace.

THE GARDEN OF PERFECT BRIGHTNESS — *YUAN MING YUAN* (OLD SUMMER PALACE)

One of the five imperial parks created during the Qing dynasty, but which is now in ruins, (popularly called the Old Summer Palace), is the Garden of Perfect Brightness. It was blown up by British and French troops in 1860 and then destroyed by fire, and only a few marble columns remain on the site, which has recently become a visitors' park with a newly dredged lake. Until 1984, when the lake was excavated, the ruins lay in farmland and were visited only by artists and young couples seeking a quiet retreat from the city. Now there is a park amusement area developing around the stone columns and the ruin of a wonderful shell-shaped fountain basin. The park is worth describing because the many western accounts of it, written in the 18th century, had a great impact on the development of European garden design. It was, by all reports, the finest of the five imperial parks beyond the city.

The Garden of Perfect Brightness was landscaped largely in the reign of the **Yong Zheng** emperor (reigned 1723–35). An adjacent garden, the Garden of Long Spring, *Chang Chun Yuan*, had been a favourite retreat of his father, the Kang Xi emperor. The gardens were later expanded and amalgamated in the reign of the Qian Long emperor so that the *Yuan Ming Yuan* ultimately included three separate gardens: the oldest garden, the Garden of Long Spring, the main complex of the Garden of Perfect Brightness, and the Garden of Joyous Spring, *Qi Chun Yuan*. All three gardens together then collectively became known as the *Yuan Ming Yuan*.

During the reign of the Qian Long emperor, European Jesuits at the imperial court were requested to design and supervise the building of palaces and fountains in a European style, in the north-east section of the garden. These palaces were built in the style of Italian Baroque but with Chinese roofs, and were surrounded by a series of fountains with mechanical pumps designed by a French Jesuit, Father Benoit. The fountains were maintained throughout the lifetime of the French missionary, but after his death the mechanisms rusted up and could not be repaired, so the court had the fountains

The ruins of the European-style palaces of the Garden of Perfect Brightness (Old Summer Palace).

An 18th century painting of a lakeside building, shaped as a Buddhist swastika, in the Garden of Perfect Brightness.

(Opposite) Plan of the Garden of Ease and Harmony — *Yi He Yuan*
1. East Palace Gate, *Dong Gong Men*
2. Hall of Benevolence and Longevity, *Ren Shou Dian*
3. Garden of Harmony and Virtue, *De He Yuan*
4. Hall of Jade Billows, *Yu Lan Tang*
5. Hall of Happiness and Longevity, *Le Shou Tang*
6. Inviting Moon Gate, *Qing Yue Men*
7. Long Gallery, *Chang Lang*
8. Marble Boat, *Shi Fang*
9. Buddha Fragrance Pagoda, *Xiang Fo Ge*
10. Temple of the Sea of Wisdom, *Zhi Hui Hai*
11. Hall that Dispels Clouds, *Pai Yun Dian*
12. Revolving Archive, *Zhuan Lun Cang*
13. Precious Clouds Pavilion, *Bao Yun Ge*
14. Garden of Harmonious Pleasures, *Xie Qu Yuan*
15. Understanding Fish Bridge, *Zhi Yu Qiao*

operated by the traditional method — hand-power.

Because these palaces and fountains were built in stone, they are all that are left of the gardens. The 1860 joint expedition by British and French troops, under the command of Lord Elgin, which was responsible for the destruction of the garden, allowed the looting of the palaces of all their treasures. The gardens were then fired upon by cannons and all the beautiful wooden halls and pavilions were engulfed in flames. Only the stone columns and fountain basins remained and, over a period of time, most of those were carried away by local people to be used as building materials.

When you look upon the ruins of the *Yuan Ming Yuan*, it is impossible to imagine the splendour of the gardens in their prime in the 18th century. However, we can gain some idea from the writings of a French Jesuit, Father Attiret, who visited these gardens quite regularly and whose accounts of them in his *Lettres Edifiantes*, published in Paris in 1749, helped to create a fashion for Chinese-style gardens in Europe. Many of his descriptions of the *Yuan Ming Yuan* seem to apply equally to the lakeside buildings of the New Summer Palace, *Yi He Yuan* and the summer resort of Chengde. There, we cannot fail to notice how carefully the Chinese master craftsmen varied their buildings in shape, size and configuration to create great diversity within small spaces as well as large.

This imperial park, like the Old Summer Palace of the *Yuan Ming Yuan*, was also burned down in 1860 by French and British troops. However, the **Empress Dowager** (lived 1835–1908) had it restored in the late 1880s as a gift to herself to celebrate her 60th birthday in 1894. The park was once again destroyed by European troops in 1900 as an act of revenge for the Boxer Rebellion in the same year, which had claimed many European lives and had led to European residents living under siege in the legation quarter. The Empress Dowager, who had fled the capital when the European powers despatched troops to capture the Qing

THE GARDEN OF EASE AND HARMONY — *YI HE YUAN* (NEW SUMMER PALACE)

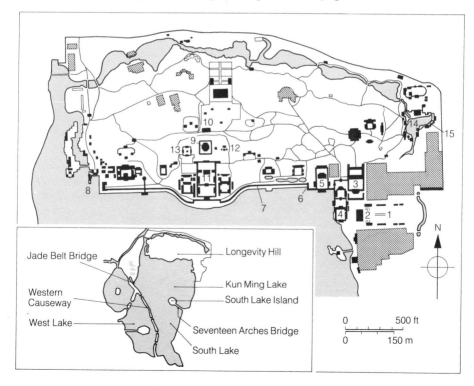

Jade Belt Bridge

Western Causeway

West Lake

Longevity Hill

Kun Ming Lake

South Lake Island

Seventeen Arches Bridge

South Lake

N

0   500 ft

0   150 m

imperial family, had the park restored again in 1902. Thus the park as we see it today has buildings which date from the late 19th and early 20th centuries with the exception of two structures on Longevity Hill which were built in the Qian Long era: the Temple of the Sea of Wisdom and the Pavilion of Precious Clouds.

The Qian Long emperor was the original architectural patron of this imperial park. Although this lake area had served as an imperial park in earlier dynasties, the palaces of these dynasties had been built around the shores of a much smaller natural lake and on a hill which stood to the north-east of the shoreline. The Qian Long emperor undertook a major hydraulic scheme which saw the enlarging of the lake and the relandscaping of the hill so that it rose gently to 60m (195ft), with its summit aligned with the central point of the northern shoreline. In order to feed the extended waters of the lake, the emperor had engineers channel water into the lake basin from the nearby Jade Spring, a few miles west of the lake. He then had the lake waters feed a series of aqueducts leading into the city so that the spring could also replenish the lakes of the Imperial City — *Beihai*, *Zhonghai* and *Nanhai* — as well as the watercourses of the Forbidden City. Thus, the lake of the imperial park was part of a complex water network that supplied water into the very heart of the capital.

In 1751, with the completion of the major landscaping work, the Qian Long emperor renamed the park the Garden of Pure Ripples, *Qing Yi Yuan*. The lake, known earlier as West Lake, *Xi Hu*, was renamed Kun Ming Lake (this was a name given to many other imperial lakes in pleasure palaces of earlier dynasties and, by tradition, is not usually translated). The hill, now extended and replanted, had its name changed from Jar Hill, *Weng Shan*, to Longevity Hill, *Wan Shou Shan*, in honour of the 60th birthday of the emperor's mother.

The names the emperor gave to the hill and the lake have remained to this day, but the name for the park, the Garden of Pure Ripples, was changed, yet again, by the Empress Dowager when she restored the park in honour of her own 60th birthday. The name she chose, the Garden of Ease and Harmony, *Yi He Yuan*, is the title by which the park is still known today.

However, in her restoration work the Empress Dowager did

not change the configuration of the park bequeathed by the Qian Long emperor. In fact, her work largely reproduced many of the buildings that had been destroyed. Yet she did allow herself one indulgence, a marble boat, rather like a Mississippi paddle steamer with Chinese details. This has become a symbol of her misrule and extravagance, for the stone paddle steamer was built with funds that had been set aside for the modernization of the Chinese imperial navy. Some may argue that in terms of the legacy to posterity, the folly in stone was the better choice. However, the boat is of no artistic interest except as a curiosity, and when I look at it I cannot help but feel sorry for the Chinese admiral who had to commit suicide on the defeat of his fleet by the Japanese navy in 1894 — an event which, ironically, led to the cancellation of the grand 60th birthday celebrations the Empress Dowager had planned for herself at the Garden of Ease and Harmony.

The lake and the hill placed centrally on its northern shoreline are the foci of the composition of this imperial park. Most of the buildings of the park, which has an area of 290ha (725 acres), are on the northern and eastern shores of the lake with the most important structures set on the southern slopes of Longevity Hill. The buildings on the eastern shore give an excellent view to the west which rises, like a Chinese painting, in three layers, from the tree-lined causeway with six bridges on the western shoreline, to the seven-storeyed slender pagoda on the summit of Jade Fountain Hill, to the distant line of the Western Hills. At sunset, this triple-layered vista is at its most effective with the hills in deep shadow and the lake tinted gold by the dying sun. It is important to remember that in the landscaping of large imperial parks, the views beyond are as important as the creation of vistas within.

Kun Ming Lake, *Kun Ming Hu*, has a circumferance of nearly 6km (4 miles) and a surface area of about 200ha (500 acres). It is divided into three distinct basins with the six-bridged Western Causeway, modelled on the Su Causeway on the West Lake at Hangzhou, separating the main lake basin from the two smaller ones. Boats and barges can enter the quiet backwaters of the two smaller lake basins by passing under one of the six bridges of the causeway. The most famous bridge of the causeway is the **Jade Belt Bridge**, *Yu Dai Qiao*, a delightful, high, single-arched white stone bridge decorated with carvings of cranes. The bridge is the major landmark of the western shoreline and is sometimes called the **Camel Hump**. Other bridges are flat or low-arched, some have pavilions and no two are the same. The causeway offers views over farm fields, beds of rushes and, in summer, deep fringes of lotus pads and flowers. The surrounding farmland once belonged to the imperial park, and the English tutor of the last emperor of China, Pu Yi (reigned 1909–12) was, for a short time, given charge of the park and farms and attempted to maintain the park with revenues collected from the farms. The tutor, Reginald Johnston, also brought his young pupil here in 1924 to learn to sail and row, much to the horror of the eunuchs who had spent their lives in service to their emperor and even tied his shoelaces!

Because the Garden of Ease and Harmony was used as a ceremonial and administrative centre as well as a resort by the Empress Dowager, it is possible to distinguish two types of architectural design within the park: official and garden. The halls around the main eastern entrance of the park were used for state business and the reception of official guests. Thus, although they have the plain, grey-blue, unglazed roof tiles of garden architecture, their woodwork is painted in the official *he xi* palace style with blue and green panels, gilded dragons and phoenixes and red pillars. Once you enter the garden precincts, you notice that the *he xi* style gives way to the *Su shi* style with pretty vignettes of birds, flowers, animals and landscapes peopled with characters from legend and fiction.

The main ceremonial hall of the park is the **Hall of Benevolence and Longevity**, *Ren Shou Dian*, which is entered through the **East Palace Gate**, *Dong Gong Men*. The gate has a formal design of three square entrances and a central imperial carriageway which depicts a dragon among clouds. The imperial carriageway dates back to the Qian Long era and was originally in the Garden of Perfect Brightness, but was moved here after the destruction of the older garden in 1860. The gateway, in keeping with its ceremonial importance, is painted in the *he xi* style.

The courtyard beyond has an impressive array of open-air bronze sculptures of sinuous dragons, phoenixes and strange-featured *qi lin*, often erroneously referred to as unicorns. There is also an impressive water-eroded rock set on a stone pedestal, which was presented to the Empress Dowager by a Manchu prince. The main hall itself has a plain, single-eaved, hip-and-gable roof in grey tiles, but in keeping with its garden surroundings has light latticed walls which extend down almost to floor level. Its interior is marked by opulent vulgarity, with two long-handled peacock feather fans and a pair of wooden carvings in the shape of the character *shou*, meaning longevity, on either side of the richly carved throne.

North of the Hall of Benevolence and Longevity is the **Garden of Harmony and Virtue**, *De He Yuan*, which is in fact an enclosed courtyard that features a three-storeyed building with an open stage on its first floor and galleries above. This stage was used for performances of Peking Opera, a traditional art form much enjoyed and patronized by the Empress Dowager. The opera is famous for its demanding singing techniques, percussive instrumentation and impressive displays of martial arts and acrobatics — the stage has several floor and ceiling traps through which gods, demons and immortals could make spectacular entrances. A well and water tank below the stage fed water spouts which could be used on the stage for special effects. Opposite the stage is the hall where the Empress Dowager sat for the performances. It is known as the **Hall of Pleasant Smiles**, *Yi Le Dian*, a reference to the Empress Dowager's enjoyment.

Other sets of halls in this eastern section of the park served as the residential quarters of the imperial family when they came to live in the park. One of the compounds, the **Hall of Jade Billows**, *Yu Lan Tang*, was where the unfortunate **Guang Xu** emperor (reigned 1875–1908) was imprisoned after the failure of the 1898 Reform Movement in which he sought political power at the expense of his much-disliked aunt, the Empress Dowager. The largest of the residential compounds is the **Hall of Happiness and Longevity**, *Le Shou Tang*, which served as the living quarters of the Empress Dowager. The compound is laid out against a gently rising slope and in its northern section has a private walled garden designed in the southern style. This style has the distinctive features of plain whitewashed walls, unadorned beamwork and decorative windows fashioned in bottle, fan and scroll shapes.

The boundary between the garden area of the park and the official and residential area is marked by a gate leading out from the west side of the compound of the Hall of Happiness and Longevity. This gate, the **Inviting Moon Gate**, *Qing Yue Men*, opens out onto a covered walkway and views over the lake. The covered walkway, known as the **Long Gallery**, *Chang Lang*, is an astonishing 728m (789yds) long and skirts the entire northern edge of the shore of the lake in a curving shape which follows the contour of the land. Small pavilions were built into the walkway so as to create a pleasant sitting area from which you can overlook the water at a particularly scenic vantage point. The whole of this covered walkway is decorated in *Su shi*-style paintings. On the interior cross beams of the walkway there are long rectangular panels with painted landscapes of scenic spots in south China, and there are scroll-edged half-moon panels that feature scenes from nature. The woodwork of the walkway is covered with more than 14,000 painted panels! In addition, the walkway becomes a living painting if you see the columns and lintels as a series of frames through which the lake and shore can be viewed.

Longevity Hill, *Wan Shou Shan* is the architectural focus of the park and on its southern slopes are set its most important buildings. These buildings are all of a religious nature and stand enclosed by a curving wall on the hillside but open to the lake on the shoreline. The groundplan for these buildings is symmetrical with a central north–south axis on which the main structures are aligned. The largest building of the complex is the **Buddha Fragrance Pagoda**, *Xiang Fo Ge*, which towers above the summit of the hill, standing at a height of 40m (130ft) on a stone platform 23m (68ft) high. A pagoda was first built here in the reign of the Qian Long emperor who had a slender nine-storeyed structure designed for the site. However, when the pagoda was nearing completion it was torn down, for a mixture of aesthetic and geomantic reasons, and was replaced with an octagonal wooden structure in three storeys and with four sets of eaves. The present structure dates from the time of the Empress Dowager's renovation work in the late 19th century, although it was modelled on the earlier Qian Long design. It is an imposing but unremarkable structure which affords excellent views over the lake to the south.

Higher up the hillside lies the **Temple of the Sea of Wisdom**, *Zhi Hui Hai*, which is approached by an immense rock pathway of unhewn stones laid out to resemble the rugged slopes of a mountain. The temple is a rectangular hall with a

double-eaved hip-and-gable roof. Its roof ridge has a wonderful sculpted frieze in glazed tiles with three small stupas at the centre. What is unusual about this hall is that it is a masonry structure, often referred to as a 'beamless hall' because it has no columns or crossbeams. Its walls are covered with glazed tiles in yellow and green, each with a recessed niche containing a Buddha image, many of which have had their faces destroyed. Contemporary Communist textbooks lay the

The Buddha Fragrance Pagoda on Longevity Hill, the Garden of Ease and Harmony.

111

The Temple of the Sea of Wisdom on Longevity Hill, the Garden of Ease and Harmony.

The Hall that Dispels Clouds at the foot of Longevity Hill, the Garden of Ease and Harmony.

blame for the damage on foreign troops, but it is likely that the building also suffered at the hands of the Red Guards in the Cultural Revolution, because the pattern of defacement is similar to the damage inflicted on other religious buildings during the years of 1966–76. The building is one of the two structures to have survived from the Qian Long era and contained a Buddha image known as the Buddha of Infinite Time.

At the foot of Longevity Hill, below the pagoda, is the main temple complex of the walled enclosure. Known as the **Hall that Dispels Clouds**, *Pai Yun Dian*, it is on the site of an earlier temple built by the Qian Long emperor in honour of his mother's 60th birthday. At that time the temple was known as the Temple of Returning Gratitude for Extended Longevity, *Da Bao En Yan Shou Si* — the Qian Long emperor was nothing if not filial. The Empress Dowager had the temple rebuilt with plans for it to be the centrepiece of her own 60th birthday celebrations. The temple complex is set around two courtyards and the buildings have roofs of yellow tiles to denote the high status of a temple founded and patronized by imperial order. The main temple hall has a double-eaved hip-and-gable roof and sits on a one-tiered stone terrace. Its woodwork is painted in the official *he xi* palace style, again to denote the temple's status as an imperial foundation. The entrance to the temple complex from the lake shore is marked by a highly elaborate three-arched ceremonial gateway, *pai lou*. On either side of the gateway is a series of 12 water-eroded rocks on stone pedestals. These are examples of open-air sculpture and each rock is said to resemble one of the 12 animals of the Chinese horoscope!

To the east and west of the Buddha Fragrance Pagoda, set amid natural rock stairways, are two sets of buildings of religious significance. The set of green-roofed pavilions to the east of the pagoda are known as the **Revolving Archive**, *Zhuan Lun Cang*, because in the central rectangular hall is a small revolving library in which the Buddhist sutras (scriptures) were stored. The roof of the hall is notable for its three glazed figurines which represent the deities of Wealth, Good Fortune and Longevity. The figure of Longevity, with his high-domed bald head, stands in the middle holding a peach in one hand

The Revolving Archive and the 1751 stele of the Qian Long emperor on Longevity Hill, the Garden of Ease and Harmony.

and with a crane by his side. Both the crane and peach are symbols of long life in China. In front of the main hall is the stone tablet, or stele, dating from 1751, on which is inscribed in the calligraphy of the Qian Long emperor the new names of the hill and lake and a brief history of the building of the lake.

On the west side of Buddha Fragrance Pagoda is the bronze pavilion known as the **Precious Clouds Pavilion**, *Bao Yun Ge*, one of the two buildings in the park to have survived from the Qian Long era. It stands on a high stone terrace surrounded by green-roofed halls and pavilions. This complex symmetrically balances the Revolving Archive complex on the east side of the enclosure. The pavilion itself is an extraordinary work of architecture for it is an imitation of a wooden pavilion, but in bronze; its brackets and beams are in bronze, and even the tiles are cast in bronze. It was here that Buddhist lamas (monks of the Tibetan sect of Buddhism) came twice a month to recite sutras on behalf of the imperial family.

On the northern wooded slopes of Longevity Hill the Qian Long emperor had built small pavilions as well as an imitation market in which eunuchs, acting out the part of the traders, sold their wares to the women of the court, whose status precluded their organizing real shopping expeditions. Most of these buildings are now in ruins. At the foot of the slopes the lake has been channelled through a narrow waterway which creates a scenic contrast to the open waters of the main body of the lake.

On the north-eastern flank of the hill the waters flow into a small lake around which a garden has been built. This garden is known as the **Garden of Harmonious Pleasures**, *Xie Qu Yuan*, and its title is taken from a poem that the Qian Long emperor wrote to celebrate his enjoyment of the place. The garden lies within a walled enclosure and was modelled on one the emperor had seen in 1751, on his travels to Wuxi, a city in south-east China. This garden, the Garden of Ease, *Ji Chang Yuan*, had been built by an official for his retirement. The emperor had his court painters make copies of vistas in the garden so that he could reproduce it within his imperial park. The garden we see today is not the garden laid out by the Qian Long emperor, but a composition from a renovation in 1811. The small lake, edged with naturally eroded rocks, is the centre of the garden. Arranged around the lake is a large number of pavilions, viewing verandahs, covered walkways and halls, set in close proximity.

The bronze ox on the eastern shore of Kun Ming Lake, the Garden of Ease and Harmony.

Within the garden is a small bridge with a name that refers to one of the great debates in Chinese philosophy. Called the **Understanding Fish Bridge**, *Zhi Yu Qiao*, the debate in question was between the Daoist master Zhuang Zi and a Confucian scholar. Zhuang Zi stood on a bridge and watched the fish in the water. He turned to his companion and said: 'Look at the fish in the water enjoying themselves.' To which his companion replied: 'How do you know they are enjoying themselves?' Zhuang Zi playfully answered this with: 'How do you know that I do not know that the fish are enjoying themselves?' Names within gardens, like the names of buildings, are rich in philosophical and literary allusions designed to enhance the enjoyment or understanding of the significance of the scene.

Another major landmark of the park is the island linked to the eastern shore of the park by a grand 17-arched bridge. Called the **South Lake Island**, *Nan Hu Dao*, it is encircled by a stone terrace which is intersected by several verandahs built out on platforms to overlook the water. The most important building on the island is the **Dragon King Temple**, *Long Wang Tang*, in which the dragon believed to control the waters of the lake was worshipped. The image of the dragon king is blue-faced. The walk around the stone terrace which encircles the island is refreshing when there is a breeze coming over the waters. The balustrade which frames the waterside terrace has pretty stone baluster caps carved in lotus form.

The 17-arched bridge to the island also has interesting carved baluster caps which depict lions, each in a different posture. The ends of the bridges are guarded by a pair of mythical beasts carved in stone with a dragon's face and a lion's mane and tail. Also on guard by the side of the lake is a beautiful, life-sized bronze statue of an ox, which was set on the eastern side of the shore by the Qian Long emperor. The side of the ox has been engraved with verse written by the Qian Long emperor. The characters are in 'seal script', the most archaic form of Chinese calligraphy, and the verse refers to the ox as a symbol used by ancient kings to tame flood waters; the emperor thus invoked the ox to protect his lake from flooding.

THE SUMMER RESORT OF CHENGDE

In the early years of the Kang Xi reign (1662–1722), civil unrest in the south-west of China prevented the emperor spending much leisure time in imperial parks. But by the first decade of the 18th century, the country was at peace and the emperor decided to build a summer resort north of the Great Wall, in an area which he had visited earlier on hunting trips. The resort was known as the Mountain Hamlet for the Escape from the Summer Heat, *Bi Shu Shan Zhuang*, and was sited in a sheltered river plain surrounded on all sides by mountains. The city that grew up around the resort is known in Chinese as Chengde.

The choice was a stroke of genius for reasons of both landscape design and military strategy. The Kang Xi emperor's forefathers had gained the throne of China through clever alliances with Mongolian chieftains, and in order to keep their loyalty, the Kang Xi emperor, too, assiduously cultivated their friendship, with official receptions at his new mountain resort. With its woods and meadows, it was far more attractive to the nomadic chieftains than the formal splendour of the halls of the Forbidden City. In terms of landscape design, the stroke of genius was to choose a river fed by warm springs as the water source for the lake at the centre of the park. The Wu Lie River, which flows into the lake, is fed by several warm springs, one of which actually rises in the north-east corner of the lake, and thus the water is ice-free through much of the winter. In fact, the Manchus called the place Jehol, which means 'Warm River'.

The Kang Xi emperor initiated the building of the resort in 1703 and construction work continued throughout the remaining 19 years of his rule. However, during the reign of his successor, the Yong Zheng emperor (reigned 1723–35), the resort was neglected, because the emperor refused to hunt and favoured the pleasures of the Garden of Perfect Harmony, *Yuan Ming Yuan* (see page 103), in the north-western district of the capital Peking. In the succeeding reign of the **Qian Long**

(Opposite) The Ford of Gathering Chestnuts, the Mountain Hamlet for the Escape from the Summer Heat.

117

A Qing dynasty illustration of riding and hunting skills at the imperial resort of Chengde.

emperor (reigned 1736–95), who greatly admired and spent much time emulating his grandfather the Kang Xi emperor, the resort was renovated. An enormous number of extra buildings was put up around the lake and in the mountain region within the enclosure of the resort. This work continued throughout the reign of the Jia Qing emperor (reigned 1796–1820), the son of the Qian Long emperor, and when he died here, after lightning set fire to the pavilion in which he was sleeping, work was still underway on new buildings. After his ill-omened death, the resort fell from favour and was not visited again by an emperor until war with European states in 1860 caused the **Xian Feng** emperor (reigned 1851–61) and his entourage to flee the capital, Peking, and come to Chengde. His death here a year later, in circumstances deemed suspicious, brought about the end of the resort as an imperial summer retreat. The Manchu monarchs who were to succeed him considered the place unlucky, and it was never again visited by an emperor. The last emperor of China, **Pu Yi** (reigned 1909–12), refused to seek sanctuary in the resort when he was forced to abdicate.

Chengde is now a small city 256km (159 miles) to the north-east of Peking. It lies outside a main section of the Great Wall, but within the outer sections of the Wall which, in this region, consist of a series of separate walls built in overlapping layers. The resort was built within an enormous walled enclosure comprising 560ha (1,384 acres) of mountain parkland, a verdant plain and a lakeland area of palaces and pavilions in the south-east. But the region was also famous for its monasteries, built out on the hillsides to the north and east of the park, and known collectively as the Eight Outer Temples.

The monasteries can be seen in the distance from within the park and are an important component of the landscape design. True to the spirit of Chinese landscape design, the natural beauty and strange rock configurations of the surrounding mountains are also elements of the landscaping of the park. On a mountaintop to the north-east sits a strange pestle-shaped rock which can be enjoyed as a 'borrowed' feature of vistas within the resort.

Because the Kang Xi and Qian Long emperors used this park for political purposes, carrying out administrative duties here as well as entertaining nomadic chieftains, the buildings around the main entrance to the park in the south-east are all official reception areas, with symmetrical hall and courtyard enclosures. However, the buildings are all built in the garden style with rustic plain roofs of grey-blue unglazed tiles. The Kang Xi emperor felt that it was unethical to be too lavish. His chosen style was studied simplicity with the tasteful combination of good as well as inexpensive materials.

THE MOUNTAIN HAMLET FOR THE ESCAPE FROM THE SUMMER HEAT — *BI SHU SHAN ZHUANG*

One of the best examples of the Kang Xi emperor's chosen style of architecture is the **Hall of Frugality and Calm**, *Dan Bo Jing Cheng Dian*, in the Main Palace complex. It is a rectangular, one-storeyed hall built out of the fragrant cedar-wood known as *nan mu*. The hall, sometimes known as Nan Mu Hall, has columns, beams and panels in expensive timber, but, like all the other buildings in the park, has a roof of plain grey tiles with a simple, floral end-of-tile motif rather than an imperial dragon. The wood throughout the hall is unpainted, the decorative touches achieved instead with carved panels and elegant light lattice frames.

In imperial times there were three palace compounds, set out on a symmetrical north–south axis, but of these only the two compounds remain: the Main Palace and the Pine and Crane Hall. Of the Eastern Palace only the grassy outline of the foundations remain. The **Main Palace**, *Zheng Gong*, is open to visitors, entered through the **Inner Meridian Gate**, *Nei Wu Men*, and has nine courtyards (nine is the number of Heaven and the creation of nine separate enclosures was a work of conscious symbolism). The smaller compound to the east, the **Pine and Crane Hall**, *Song He Zhai*, is currently off-

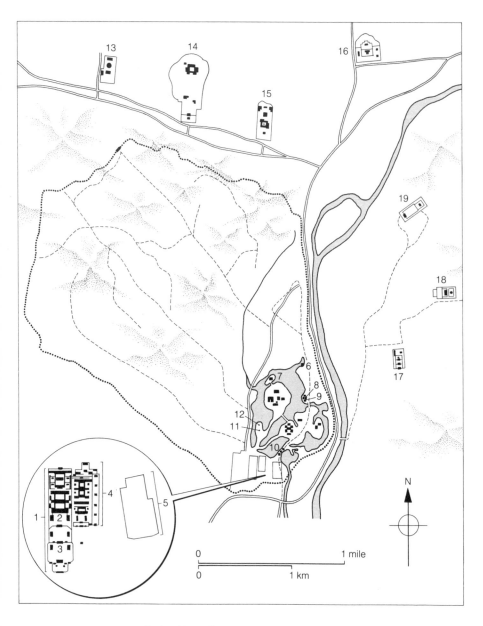

limits. The pine and crane are both symbols of longevity and this palace area was built by the Qian Long emperor for his mother as a palace of retirement in her old age.

It is possible to stroll through the nine courtyards of the Main Palace, leave the compound through the northern gate and walk down a wooded hillside to enter the park area. The parkland is vast: the resort is twice the size of the Garden of Ease and Harmony (see page 105), and eight times the size of Beihai Park in Peking (see page 78). Within the crenellated battlements of the park walls, which have a perimeter of 100km (6 miles), there are three distinctive areas of landscape: the wooded hills to the west, the grassy plain to the north, and the lake and its pavilions to the south-east. In imperial times, there were a large number of buildings including hilltop pavilions, small temples and enclosed courtyards set amid the wooded hills in the western section of the park. Some were built as rest lodges for those enjoying walks on the mountain paths. Others served as look-out pavilions from which visitors could enjoy fine views over the lake below, the surrounding mountains and the bright colours of the distant roofs of the mountain monasteries. Today very few of these hillside and hilltop buildings remain: most fell into a state of disrepair in the 19th century when the imperial family no longer lavished money on the upkeep of the resort.

The grassy plain and low woodland in the northern section of the park were once a hunting reserve and place for great outdoor feasts in the time of the Kang Xi and Qian Long emperors. It was here that the Mongolian chieftains were fêted and flattered into loyal submission to the dragon throne of China. Sadly, this area is now disfigured by rows of ugly, utilitarian buildings and where tents were once set up by the emperors to enjoy open-air entertaining, there is now the most grotesque 'yurtel', or compound of yurts (circular nomadic tents), in which visitors can stay overnight. Pop music blasts out of speakers around the compound and a great central yurt is used as a dance hall! The slender nine-storeyed pagoda, commissioned by the Qian Long emperor, that dominates this area of the park is currently being restored.

The lakeland area of the resort is the finest part of the park and has been better preserved than the more outlying sections. The lake itself has none of the open grandeur of the Kun Ming Lake in the Garden of Ease and Harmony, but instead has a complex pattern of islands and causeways which breaks it into seven distinct basins. However, it is difficult to imagine the

(Opposite) Plan of the Mountain Hamlet for the Escape from the Summer Heat and the Eight Outer Temples

Palace Area
1. Main Palace, *Zheng Gong*;
2. Hall of Frugality and Calm, *Dan Bo Jing Cheng Dian*;
3. Inner Meridian Gate, *Nei Wu Men*;
4. Pine and Crane Hall, *Song He Zhai*;
5. Eastern Palace, *Dong Gong* (ruins);

Lake Area
6. Warm River Spring, *Re He Quan*;
7. Hall of Mists and Rain, *Yan Yu Lou*;
8. Golden Mountain, *Jin Shan* (promontary of land);
9. Tower of God, *Shang Di Lou* (main building of *Jin Shan*);
10. Pavilions in the Heart of the Water, *Shui Xin Xie*;
11. Surrounded by Azure, *Huan Bi*;
12. Ford of Gathering Chestnuts, *Cai Ling Du*;

Eight Outer Temples
13. Temple of the Image of Manjusri, *Shu Xian Si*;
14. Temple of the Potala, *Pu Tuo Zong Cheng Miao*;
15. Temple of Sumeru Happiness and Longevity, *Xu Mi Fu Shou Miao*;
16. Temple of Universal Peace, *Pu Ning Si*;
17. Temple of Universal Sincerity, *Pu Ren Si*;
18. Temple of Universal Happiness, *Pu Le Si*;
19. Temple of Distant Peace, *An Yuan Si*.

original configuration of the shoreline, because the lake has silted up and is now only two-thirds of its former size.

The network of causeways was modelled on the famous causeways of the West Lake in Hangzhou, visited and admired by both the Kang Xi and Qian Long emperors. Both emperors each designed 36 scenic vantage spots within the park and wrote poems to celebrate the beauty of each place. It is now difficult to visualize these beauty spots as they looked in imperial times, because the lack of garden maintenance and the wear and tear of a multitude of visitors have left the park in a shabby state. Yet in the early morning, when a mist is still on the water and the visitors have yet to arrive in their busloads, the lake remakes its magic.

Spring comes early in this sheltered mountain valley, and when the rest of the North China Plain is still dun and dry in its winter colours, here the trees are already in bud. Even the winter is delayed here because the warmth of the spring water in the lake allows the lotuses to flower through the early autumn. All these aspects of the resort must have made it a wonderful retreat from the rigours of the Peking climate and the ceaseless round of official ceremonies and sacrifices undertaken during the winter months in the Forbidden City. The Kang Xi and Qian Long emperors had little love of the palaces of their capital and spent, on average, only three months a year within the Forbidden City. Those three months, which covered the Winter Solstice ceremonies and the lunar New Year, were a period of important imperial rituals and the retreat to the hunting grounds of Chengde must have been a welcome relief.

There are many famous buildings around the lake, the most celebrated of which is the double-storeyed **Hall of Mists and Rain**, *Yan Yu Lou*, which overlooks the northern shore of the lake from a small island linked to the shore by bridges. This is considered the main building of the lake area and is an attractive plain rectangular structure with a simple single-eaved, hip-and-gable roof. The hall has no polychromatic painted beamwork, unlike the buildings of the Peking imperial parks, but has instead plain red painted woodwork which contrasts attractively with the grey tiles of the roof and the white stone of the surrounding terrace.

On the eastern shore of the lake is **Golden Mountain**, *Jin*

Shan, a small artificial hill of a landscaped rockery crowned with a three-storeyed hexagonal pagoda. The pagoda, known as the **Tower of God**, *Shang Di Lou*, is a wooden structure which has a lightness of composition, created by the open galleries that surround each of its three storeys. Beneath the pagoda lies a set of halls and pavilions with an open-walled covered walkway which skirts the curved shoreline. Golden Mountain was built in 1703 by order of the Kang Xi emperor who wished it to be modelled on the Golden Mountain Temple, *Jin Shan Si*, in the city of Zhenjiang in Jiangsu province. This temple was visited by the emperor on one of his imperial tours. He was so struck by the beauty of the original Golden Mountain Temple, which commands a fine view over the Yangzi River, that he wrote a eulogy of the temple which was inscribed in stone and displayed within the temple. The Qian Long emperor, during his southern tours, was, like his grandfather, also struck by the beauty of the temple and commanded a stone inscription with his verses of praise to be set up alongside his grandfather's stele.

The Tower of God on Golden Mountain, the Mountain Hamlet for the Escape from the Summer Heat.

Another famous feature of the lakeland area, the three pavilions known as the **Pavilions in the Heart of the Water**, *Shui Xin Xie*, were also inspired by the architecture of the Yangzi region, this time the West Lake of Hangzhou. These three pavilions were commissioned by the Qian Long emperor and were designed as one of his 36 beauty spots. The pavilions

The Pavilions in the Heart of the Water, the Mountain Hamlet for the Escape from the Summer Heat.

all have double-eaved roofs with plain grey tiles. The central pavilion is rectangular and the identical pair of side pavilions are square in form. All three pavilions have open sides from which the views over the water were to be enjoyed. Under the central pavilion lies a sluice gate which was used to control the water levels between the central and side lakes.

There are many other famous beauty spots around the lake, but my favourite is the 13th of the 36 scenic spots of the Qian Long emperor. It lies on a small island called **Surrounded by Azure**, *Huan Bi*, in the south-west corner of the lake, and is called the **Ford of Gathering Water Chestnuts**, *Cai Ling Du*. It was here that the emperor came accompanied by his consorts to watch the harvesting of the water chestnuts which grow in the mud at the fringes of the lake. Here you will see a small collection of simple rustic-style halls and pavilions, one of which has a charming, irregularly shaped courtyard with whitewashed walls built in gentle wavelike curves. A small covered walkway with open sides runs down from the halls to the edge of the water and ends at a promontory on which

124

stands a simple circular pavilion with a thatched roof. This park has none of the grand and brightly coloured architecture of the other remaining imperial parks in Peking; here the buildings blend more subtly and more naturally with the landscape.

All of the 'Eight' Outer Temples lie on the lower slopes of the mountains to the north and east of the imperial park, the Mountain Hamlet for the Escape from the Summer Heat. Both the Kang Xi and Qian Long emperors were the patrons of the temples and by the end of the Qian Long era, a total of 12 major foundations had been commissioned, eight of which were funded from the imperial treasury and the rest by private donations and rents. Only seven of the eight imperial temples remain today and all but one date from the Qian Long era. In the northern mountain region lie the largest and later temples: The Temple of the Image of Manjusri, built in 1774 in the 39th year of the Qian Long reign; the Temple of the Potala, built in 1771 in the 36th year of the Qian Long reign (and the year of the emperor's 60th birthday); the Temple of Sumeru Happiness and Longevity, built in 1780, in the 45th year of the Qian Long reign and the year of the emperor's 70th birthday; and the Temple of Universal Peace, built in 1755, the 20th year of the Qian Long era. In the eastern mountains there are three

THE EIGHT OUTER TEMPLES — *WAI BA MIAO*

View of the predominantly Tibetan style architecture of the Temple of the Potala, Eight Outer Temples.

surviving temples, the earliest of which, the Temple of Universal Sincerity, dates from 1713, the 52nd year of the Kang Xi reign. The Temple of Universal Happiness dates from 1766, the 31st year of the Qian Long reign and the nearby Temple of Distant Peace was built in 1764, the 29th year of the Qian Long era.

The temples, as much as the park, were built as a political exercise in forging alliances of loyalty and respect between the Manchu ruling house and the nomadic warriors of Mongolia and Chinese-controlled Central Asia. The Kang Xi emperor initiated this process, but his temples were built in the traditional Han Chinese style with the conventional assembly of symmetrical courtyards. The **Temple of Universal Sincerity**, *Pu Ren Si*, is the only surviving temple from this era and is currently not officially open to visitors.

The Qian Long emperor was more imaginative and more extravagant than his predecessor in his approach to temple building, and created monasteries which were replicas in miniature of the famous monasteries of Mongolia, Central Asia, Tibet and other temples in China. In fact, most of the temples built in the Qian Long era take their inspiration from Lamaism, the Tibetan sect of Buddhism.

The **Temple of the Potala**, *Pu Tuo Zong Cheng Miao*, is the largest of these temples, and was patterned on the Dalai Lama's Potala Palace in the capital of Tibet, Lhasa. The Qian Long emperor, who was intensely religious (as can be seen from the Buddhist images carved in his coffin crypt), hoped that the Dalai Lama would come personally to visit him and built this temple in which to receive him.

The Dalai Lama never did visit the court of the Qian Long emperor, but the Panchen Lama did in 1779 (the Panchen Lama is a senior lama, or monk teacher, who is an incarnation of a Buddhist deity and second only to the Dalai Lama in Tibetan Buddhism). The **Temple of Sumeru Happiness and Longevity**, *Xu Mi Fu Shou*, was built in honour of his visit, and was in fact modelled on the Panchen Lama's own monastery, the Tashilhunpo in Shigatse, the second city of Tibet.

In the early years of his reign, the Qian Long emperor sent draughtsmen to Tibet to make drawings of famous lamaseries. From the drawings, the emperor chose the five-roofed hall of the Samye-Ling monastery in Tibet as the model for the main

hall of the **Temple of Universal Peace**, *Pu Ning Si*. The hall has a deep 'well-shaft' ceiling in order to house a 22m (72ft) high statue of a 'Thousand-armed Bodhisattva of Mercy'. The statue has in fact got 42 arms and is the largest extant wooden statue in China.

The fourth of the Qian Long's temples, the **Temple of the Image of Manjusri**, *Shu Xian Si*, was badly destroyed by artillery fire in the 1960s and is currently closed to the public.

In all of the Tibetan-inspired temples commissioned by the Qian Long emperor, you will see an extraordinary blend of Chinese and Tibetan architecture. The wooden halls and pavilions, the arched masonry gates with glazed tile roofs and the formal layout of buildings round a courtyard, all have their roots in Chinese architecture. But the large masonry walls (which are not perpendicular and taper inwards as they rise), the blind windows, and the scatter of differently shaped stone and brick buildings set around the hillside, all derive from Tibetan building traditions. The altitude, extreme temperature fluctuations and high winds of Tibet make the climate extremely inhospitable and such sturdy buildings with few windows were necessary to make life bearable in the cold Himalayan highlands.

The decorative motifs of these Lamaist temples are also

The Temple of Sumeru Happiness and Longevity: the main temple hall is square with a distinctive gilded roof featuring eight roof ridge flood dragons, Eight Outer Temples.

127

A glazed ceramic stupa. Eight Outer Temples.

different from the traditional designs of Chinese architecture. The different-coloured glazed stupas, which are a feature above masonry gateways and on roof platforms, represent the four major and four minor continents in Buddhist cosmography. The stupas, an Indian architectural form known as *chhörten* in Tibet, stand as symbols of salvation. Stupas vary in shape and colour but usually conform to the basic structure of a pot-shaped form set on a square base, topped with 'umbrellas' and symbols for the Sun and Moon. Also, at the ends of the eaves of many of the main temple halls there are Tibetan 'water dragons': dragon-faced, elephant-nosed creatures which guard the corners of the roof. Under these hang small wind bells. Rafter ends are decorated with Sanskrit letters and the Buddhist swastika rather than the secular, Chinese, designs of coloured circles, flowers or longevity symbols.

On the foothills of the mountains to the east of the park are two famous temples which are totally unalike. The first is the Chinese-style **Temple of Universal Happiness**, *Pu Le Si*, which has a main hall with a double-eaved, conical roof which, in shape, resembles the Hall for Good Harvests in the Temple of Heaven complex in Peking. However, unlike the blue-tiled roof of the Hall of Good Harvests, the **Dawn Light Hall**, *Xu Guang Dian*, has roof tiles in the imperial yellow colour. Also, inside this Chinese-style building is a very un-Chinese Tantric statue of a deity in a position of sexual intercourse — an act which symbolizes the synthesis of supreme knowledge and compassion.

A detail of a Tibetan-style roof end decoration of water dragons. Eight Outer Temples.

The second of these temples, the **Temple of Distant Peace**, *An Yuan Si*, a rectangular black-roofed hall lies on an adjoining slope of the mountain. The black tiles of the hall are unusual for a Chinese religious building, although the shape of the building itself is completely Chinese; this is because the temple was built as a replica of a Buddhist foundation, the Guerzha Temple, in the city of Ili in Chinese Central Asia. Take a torch to see the wonderful murals inside this temple, which depict stories from the Buddhist scriptures.

Although the Kang Xi and Qian Long emperors had temples built on the hillsides outside their park to forge close political and religious links with their fellow nomadic peoples, they were not unaware of the role of the temples in the landscape of the park as a whole. From the high points in the

wooded mountain area inside the park, it is possible to look out over the mountains and see the glazed tiles of the temple roofs gleaming in the sun; there is a great variety in the views, for all the temples have different and distinctive features in their layout, colour schemes and balance and sequence of roof heights.

The distinctive black-roofed, rectangular Temple of Distant Peace, the Eight Outer Temples.

Of the Eight Outer Temples some fell into decay in the 19th century; others were the victims of the civil war that engulfed

The main temple hall of the Temple of Universal Peace houses the 'Thousand Armed Bodhisattva of Mercy'. Eight Outer Temples.

China for the greater part of the first half of this century. The Japanese occupation of China in the Second World war, too, led to highly discriminate looting (many Japanese are Buddhists with a liking for religious works of art). The 1966–1976 Cultural Revolution and its anti-religious and anti-traditional fervour also led to the jolly practice of the Chinese army using some of the temples as targets for artillery exercises. Dynamite and mortar finished off what neglect and rain had started. Money is being spent on the temples at present and much still remains to be done.

Most of the Eight Outer Temples are now being restored, except for the Temple of Universal Peace, where restoration work was recently completed. Some of the temples are either completely closed to visitors, or have sections which are off-limits. A combination of luck and persuasion often gains the visitor a glimpse of restoration work underway. But sadly, most of the religious treasures have long since gone. What do remain, however, are wonderfully inventive buildings, rare murals and the great statues, which, thankfully, were too heavy to carry away. Nowhere else in China has such a rich diversity of religious architecture within such a small area. The temples well deserve a volume of their own.

The Temple of Universal Happiness, Eight Outer Temples.

THE IMPERIAL TOMBS

Interestingly, the Chinese had a similar view of the afterlife to that of the ancient Egyptians: it was a place where the spirit had the same needs as the body in the material world. Chinese rulers, like Egyptian Pharoahs, were buried with treasures, household utensils, images of favourite servants and animals and, in the very early period of Chinese civilization as well as the early years of the Ming dynasty (1368–1644), with members of the emperor's household who were usually forced to commit suicide. Traditional Chinese cosmology had no place like the Heaven of Christianity where the soul is freed from its earthly desires. Even emperors who were devout Buddhists, such as the Qian Long emperor (reigned 1736–95), went to their tombs with beautiful artefacts in lacquer, porcelain, jade, silver, gold and silk. The tradition of ancestor worship also ensured that the spirits of the departed were honoured, with burnt offerings of silk and money as well as sacrifices of animals and wine. Such sacrifices had to be maintained in order for the ancestors to bestow their blessings on their descendants. These elaborate preparations for tomb building and burial were a necessary part of the pattern of ritual behaviour which maintained the link between the living and the dead.

Tombs are the richest source of material information we have on imperial China. The first emperor of China, Qin Shi Huang Di (reigned 221–10 BC), who united the small warring states of late Zhou China in 221 BC, was interred in a large square underground tomb which has yet to be opened by archaeologists. Near to his tomb, at Xian, was buried the fabulous army of larger-than-life terracotta warriors whose images were sent into the ground to guard the emperor in the spirit world. Many tombs of the Han dynasty (206 BC–AD 220) are known to archaeologists; their underground chambers have proved to be treasure houses of precious works of art which would have had little chance of surviving into this era had they not been buried with the dead.

(Opposite) The ceramic furnace at Chang Ling, tomb of the Ming emperor Yong Le. It was in these furnaces that sacrifices of silk and money were burnt for the dead emperor.

133

Tomb building and burial practices varied over the many succeeding dynasties, but there were certain constants in the burial of emperors. We know that emperors usually commissioned their tombs in their lifetime and often took a personal interest in their mausoleums. Coffins of wood were invariably used and these, along with wooden boxes full of precious objects and household items, were buried in underground vaults. The vaults were always of brick or stone, although very frugal and conscientious emperors were known to have requested simple burials in the earth. The arrangement of the underground vaults varied greatly over the imperial period, from single vaults to a series of interconnected chambers. The emperor was usually buried in the same tomb, but not necessarily the same tomb chamber, as his empresses and favoured concubines. These arrangements could be changed after an emperor's death if the next emperor was the son of a concubine who had not been buried with the deceased emperor. Filial sons often reorganized the tomb of their deceased father when they became emperors, either to settle old scores or to please a demanding mother. It seems that children were never buried with their parents. Concubines often had their own tombs, on a modest scale, outside the tomb enclosure of the emperor but usually in the same valley.

Tomb siting and building were important activities in the imperial household, and civil servants from the Board of Rites, one of the six imperial ministries, were entrusted to make sure that tombs were constructed with the degree of dignity demanded by the future occupant and with the best possible geomantic forces at work on the site. Preferred sites always faced towards the south, were sheltered from behind by high ground, commanded a good view and had a watercourse flowing in front of the tomb entrance. Strict symmetry was observed in the building, of the sacrificial halls in front of the tomb entrance. It was to these halls that the descendants of the emperor would come, on the anniversary of his birth and death, as well as on important ceremonial dates in the lunar calendar, to make offerings to his spirit.

Because no ceremonial halls, the above-ground architecture of imperial tombs, remain from the pre-Ming era, this chapter will discuss the tombs of the Ming and Qing periods only. The founding emperor of the Ming dynasty, the Hong Wu emperor

(reigned 1368–98), is buried outside Nanjing in the Purple and Gold Mountains. No buildings from the tomb enclosure remain, because the tomb was destroyed and looted during the Taiping Rebellion in the mid-19th century. All subsequent Ming emperors, with the exception of two who were ousted in palace coups, are buried to the north of Peking, in the valleys that we know as the Ming Tombs and which the Chinese call *Shi San Ling*, which means the Thirteen Mausolea, for the thirteen emperors buried on the site.

The corner towers and three-storeyed ceremonial hall of Zhao Ling, the tomb of Abahai, the Manchu overlord, at Bei Ling, the northern Qing tombs in Shenyang.

The founding ruler of the Qing imperial house, **Abahai** (reigned 1626–43), who never actually ruled from Peking but consolidated Manchu power in the north, is buried with his wife outside Shenyang, the early Manchu capital. His tomb, known as the Northern Mausoleum, *Bei Ling*, is a 180,000m² (216,000yd²) enclosure in the northern suburbs of the city of Shenyang in Liaoning province. Buildings at the Northern Mausoleum are in a good state of repair and the tomb has a much more military style of architecture than the tombs of later Qing emperors. The Northern Mausoleum has a set of four corner towers above the high-walled rectangular enclosure in front of the tomb mound. These decorative corner towers were not repeated in subsequent imperial tombs.

All later Qing emperors, with the exception of the last emperor, were buried to the east and west of Peking, in the two great tomb areas known as the Eastern Tombs, *Dong Ling*, and

Western Tombs, *Xi Ling*. The Eastern Tombs are the more important complex, containing the tombs of five emperors. The Western Tombs now cover a larger area but include only four emperors' tombs. The three major tomb sites — the Ming Tombs, the Eastern Tombs and the Western Tombs — are all in settings of great natural beauty. The emperors of China, like the most humble Chinese peasants, wished for their tomb sites to have the most auspicious geomantic forces associated with the felicitous combinations of mountains, verdant valleys and streams. However, unlike the humble peasants who had to make do with their local hillside, emperors had an empire at their disposal when it came to looking for tomb sites.

Tomb Architecture

Because it is not possible within the confines of this book to give details of every imperial tomb in the three major tomb sites, it seems best to give a general description of tomb architecture and to then focus on tombs which have some particular feature of great architectural interest. Many of the tombs are in a state of great decay and it is only the tombs of exceptional size or architectural interest that have been maintained over the years. The Qing emperors, who in all they did showed enthusiasm and pride in their adherence to imperial orthodoxy, took great pains to keep the Ming tombs in good order out of respect for their predecessors. Today, restoration work is currently underway at all three tomb complexes, and tomb halls are being completely rebuilt on their foundations. One of these is the *Zhao Ling*, the tomb of the **Long Qing** (reigned 1567–72), emperor of the Ming dynasty. An American timber company has sponsored the restoration of the tomb and quality timber from the United States of America is being used in a complete reconstruction of the main sacrificial halls of the tomb complex.

In imperial times, tomb complexes were surrounded by red, green and white marker posts and had special garrisons assigned to protect them. Because of the importance of the ancestors in giving blessings to their descendants, their tombs had to be guarded against attack and desecration. Within the vast acres of the tomb complexes, no one was allowed to till the soil, cut down trees or gather wood. Villages in the vicinity of

Plan of a tomb enclosure.

- Coffin crypt
- Crypt antechamber
- Entrance to underground crypt
- Circular earth mound covering underground tomb
- Bright Tower *Ming Lou*
- Open-air stone altar
- Main sacrificial hall
- Side halls
- Ceramic funerary ovens
- Gate
- N
- Stele pavilion
- Watercourse
- Set of bridges

the tombs had a duty to guard and maintain the tomb enclosures and were rewarded from the imperial treasury. No visitor to the tombs was allowed to go on horseback within the tomb complex.

The tomb sites designated by the early emperors are the largest and most dominant in terms of landscaping. Out of filial respect and the wish not to upstage their ancestors' achievements, successors usually built more modest tomb complexes. However, there were emperors who, having achieved long reign periods and presided over peaceful and prosperous times, went in for a little self-congratulation with large and well-built tombs. Emperors whose lives were short or troubled by wars and economic crises often had to be laid to rest in hastily erected mausolea, or, in the case of the last emperor of the Ming dynasty, in the tomb of a concubine who had predeceased him.

The main ceremonial stone archway marking the main entrance to the Eastern Qing tombs.

The main dynastic stele of the Ming house at the Ming tombs which describes the glories and achievements of the Ming rulers.

There are three distinct elements in imperial tomb architecture: the approach to the tomb, the buildings in front of the tomb mound, and the underground chamber. Each imperial tomb complex has a central approach, and each individual tomb with a greater or lesser degree of grandeur, also has its own approach. A ceremonial stone archway on a grand scale, with five arches, marks the beginning of the central approach to the imperial tombs. Next comes a large three-arched, masonry gateway, behind which stands a masonry 'Stele Pavilion' which houses a large stone memorial tablet, or stele. The tablet is the main record of the tombs of the complex. In addition, each tomb has its own stele which records the achievements of the individual emperor. The main Stele Pavilion has two pairs of white, carved stone columns, or *hua biao*, (see page 53) on either side of it.

After the Stele Pavilion you reach the 'Spirit Avenue'. This is the ceremonial pathway along which the coffin was carried to its last resting place. On either side of this ceremonial pathway stand large stone statues of animals, mythological beasts, military and civil officials to guard and bring good fortune to the spirit of the deceased emperor. In the Ming Tombs there is one main Spirit Avenue which approaches the web of valleys over which the imperial tombs are spread. In the Eastern Qing tombs, there is a main spirit avenue and also three smaller spirit avenues which lead to the individual tombs of the Kang Xi (reigned 1662–1722), Qian Long and **Xian Feng** (reigned 1851–61) emperors.

Tombs built on a small scale by emperors who either chose

The main Spirit Avenue of the Eastern Qing tombs. The Spirit Avenue features two pairs of each animal: one pair kneeling and one pair standing. After the animals there are pairs of standing military and civilian officials.

not to spend much on their mausolea or died before they could have their tombs designed, have a simple entrance with a gateway into a walled enclosure.

The individual tombs can have one, two or three courtyards in front of the burial mound. The grandest tombs of the Ming emperor Yong Le (reigned 1402–24) and Wan Li (reigned 1573–1620) both have a sequence of three courtyards. In the tomb buildings in front of the underground chamber certain elements were obligatory: small ceramic funerary ovens in which sacrificial offerings of silk and money were burned; side halls in which the preparation for the sacrifices at the tomb could be made; a main hall in which ancestral sacrificial ceremonies took place; an open-air stone altar on which stood the standard set of five sacred vessels carved in stone — two candlesticks, two flower vases and a central incense burner. The entrance to the circular walled enclosure of the earth mound covering the underground burial chamber was usually marked by a masonry tower, double-eaved with a hip-and-gable roof and set on top of a brick and stone platform. This tower is known as a Bright Tower, *Ming Lou*, and guarded the entrance to the underground vault. The **Dao Guang** emperor (reigned 1821–50) chose not to have a Bright Tower built at his mausoleum in the Western Qing Tombs. The burial chamber itself was always built underground as a single or series of brick and stone vaults and was covered over with a large mound of earth.

Most tombs of emperors were opened several times to accommodate the coffins of empresses and concubines, but the underground vaults had enormous stone doors with an ingenious self-locking device that made the tomb difficult to enter unless opened by the craftsman who had worked on its construction. Many of China's imperial tombs, especially from the pre-Ming period have been looted, but, astonishingly, the majority of the Ming and Qing tombs have yet to be excavated. However, one tomb of the late imperial period that has been looted is that of the **Empress Dowager** (lived 1835–1908), the *Ding Dong Ling*, of the Eastern Tombs. It was looted in the Republican era by a local warlord, and many of its fabulous treasures were distributed among the corrupt generals of the Kuomintang, who at that time were ruling China under the leadership of Chiang Kai Shek. Madame Chiang Kai Shek is reputed to have acquired many of the 33,560 fabulous pearls buried with the Empress Dowager.

THE MING TOMBS — *SHI SAN LING*

The 13 tombs of the Ming emperors lie in a fertile river valley in Chang Ping county 50km (31 miles) to the north of Peking. The tombs are scattered over an area of 40km² (15 square miles) and not all are visible from the main approach. Many of the tombs are situated on the slopes of subsidiary valleys which reach, like fingers, up into the surrounding mountains. The tombs have been built in sympathy with the landscape of the valley and make use of rising land and hillocks to place the buildings in a focal point of the setting. Apart from the tombs of the 13 emperors, there are also the tombs of a large number of concubines scattered round the valleys. Also, within the enclosure of the Ming tombs lies the grave mound of a eunuch, Wang Cheng En, who in 1644 committed suicide with his master, the Chong Zhen emperor (reigned 1628–44), the last of the Ming line.

The **Spirit Avenue** of the Ming Tombs is perhaps the most famous landmark of the tomb complex and well deserves description. A total of 36 statues line the avenue, not including the pair of hexagonal stone columns, *wang zhu*, that mark the start of the avenue and that were believed to guide the soul of the emperor to its resting place. Of the 36 statues, which were carved in the 15th century, 24 are of animals and 12 of humans. The statues stand in identical pairs, one of each pair on either

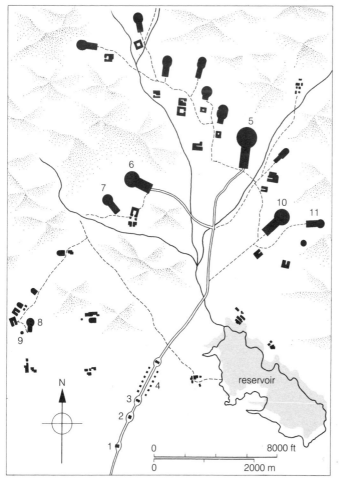

Plan of Ming Tombs
1. Ceremonial archway;
2. Great Red Gate;
3. Great Stele Pavilion;
4. Spirit Avenue;
5. *Chang Ling* tomb of the Yong Le emperor;
6. *Ding Ling* tomb of the Wan Li emperor;
7. *Zhao Ling* tomb of the Long Qing emperor;
8. *Si Ling* tomb of the Chong Zhen emperor;
9. Tomb of the Eunuch Wang Cheng En;
10. *Yong Ling* tomb of the Jia Jing emperor;
11. *De Ling* tomb of the Tian Qi emperor.

side of the avenue. There are two pairs of each animal: one pair in the kneeling position and one pair standing.

All the animals, except for two, are recognizable as real creatures. The two mythical creatures are the *xie zhi*, a feline beast with a flowing mane and a central protruberance on its forehead, and the *qi lin*, a beast with a scaly body, a flowing mane and cloven hooves. Both these mythical beasts were believed to have spiritual powers and the *xie zhi* was said to be able to divine right from wrong. The 12 human figures are of four military officers, four civilian officials and four ministers, all dressed in ceremonial garments that would have

A statue of an army general in the Spirit Avenue of the Ming Tombs.

been worn in the presence of the emperor. The total length of the Spirit Avenue, from the memorial arch to the gate of the tomb of the Yong Le emperor, is 7km (4.5 miles). In accordance with the demands of traditional geomancy, it is built on a curved line.

The main tomb of the complex, *Chang Ling*, is the **mausoleum of the Yong Le emperor**, and has yet to be excavated. The above-ground complex of buildings are all in a good state of repair having been recently renovated. The mausoleum is now a major tourist attraction and houses, somewhat inappropriately, jolly sideshows, tourist shops and photographic booths featuring painted warriors and maidens. Nevertheless, none of this detracts from the grandeur of the main sacrificial hall of the tomb complex. The hall, known as the **Hall of Eminent Favours**, *Ling En Dian* (a name given to all the sacrificial halls of the Ming tombs), is one of the finest pieces of Ming architecture to have survived to this day. It is a rectangular wooden structure measuring 66.6m (217ft) from east to west and 29.3m (95ft) from north to south. The roof, built in the grand double-eaved hip style, is supported by 32 immense single columns of *nan mu*, a costly fragrant cedarwood from the south of China. These columns are each made from a single trunk and rise to a height of 14.3m (over 46ft). In late imperial China, the scarcity and cost of such wood made such buildings with *nan mu* columns an increasingly rare occurrence. The interior of the hall is remarkable for its complex tiers of brackets, *dou gong*, which in this building serve both a functional and decorative purpose.

The other main attraction at the Ming Tombs is the *Ding Ling*, the **tomb of the Wan Li emperor**, which had its burial chamber opened by state archaeologists in the 1950s. Walking through the underground vaults you can gain some idea of the scale and expense involved in building imperial tombs. The artefacts buried with the Wan Li emperor's coffin are now on display in the *Chang Ling*, the tomb of the Yong Le emperor, in the main sacrificial hall, the *Ling En Dian*. The tomb treasures are splendid and only serve to make one wonder what is buried in the unexcavated tombs of other emperors.

Most of the other tombs of the Ming emperors are open to visitors (above ground, but not below), except where restoration work is underway. Tombs under repair need special

The Bright Tower of Ding Ling, the tomb of the Ming emperor Wan Li.

permits to be visited; these have to be applied for in Peking at the Cultural Relics Bureau. Tour buses visit the tombs regularly, but guided tours tend to whisk visitors round the tombs too quickly and spend too much time helping them to lighten their purses at the restaurant and well-stocked tourist shops. The best way to see the tombs is to hire a taxi in the city centre and keep it for the day. The taxi driver, if friendly, is usually willing to take you to explore the more remote tombs. If you are on a budget holiday, the best plan is to go to the tombs by local bus and then hire a bicycle to enable you to see as much as possible in one day.

The Eastern Qing Tombs are 125km (78 miles) east of Peking and cover an area of 48km² (17 square miles). The original area of the tombs in the imperial period was 2,500km² (950 miles²). There are a total of 15 tombs here of which five are the tombs of emperors — the Shun Zhi emperor, *Xiao Ling*; the Kang Xi emperor, *Jing Ling*; the Qian Long emperor, *Yu Ling*; the Xian Feng emperor (reigned 1851–61), *Ding Ling*; and the Tong Zhi emperor (reigned 1862–74), *Hui Ling*. Also of note are the twin tombs of the Kang Xi concubines with their green-roofed 'Bright Towers' and the parallel yellow-roofed *Ding Dong Ling*,

THE EASTERN QING TOMBS — *DONG LING*

Map of the Eastern
Qing Tombs
1. Ceremonial
Archway;
2. Great Red Gate;
3. Stele Pavilion;
4. Spirit Avenue;
5. *Xiao Ling* tomb of
the Shun Zhi emperor;
6. *Yu Ling* tomb of
the Qian Long
emperor;
7. *Ding Ling* tomb of
the Xian Feng
emperor;
8. *Ding Dong Ling*
double tomb of the
two empresses of the
Xian Feng emperor;
9. *Jing Ling* tomb of
the Kang Xi emperor;
10. Double tomb of
the Kang Ki emperor's
concubines;
11. *Hui Ling* tomb of
the Tong Zhi emperor.

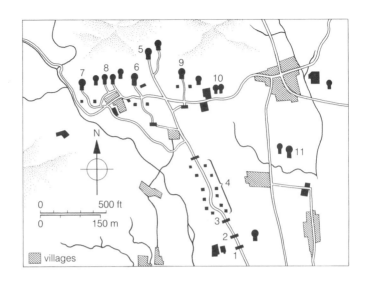

the tombs of the two empresses of the Xian Feng emperor.

I first visited these tombs 11 years ago on a university
excursion, when they were not open to tourists and have fond
memories of the landscape there. Even today, the tombs are an
unusually pleasant place for a day's outing because they do not
attract crowds and their setting against towering mountains
and fertile farmland makes them more attractive than the
heavily commercialized Ming tombs, where there are plans
afoot to build leisure centres. The tombs, many of which are
not open to the public, still have the air of quiet tranquillity
that allows one to picture the setting before farmers were
allowed to till the sacred lands and cut down the trees of the
enclosure. Most of the tombs are visible from the main
approach, and the mixture of yellow and green-glazed roofs
(yellow for the emperors and empresses' tombs and green for
the tombs of the concubines) makes an attractive vista from
the Spirit Avenue that leads to the first tomb of the complex,
Xiao Ling, the **mausoleum of the Shun Zhi emperor** (reigned
1644–61). He was the first Manchu leader to rule from Peking,
and the founder of the Qing dynasty.

The underground chamber of the *Yu Ling*, the **tomb of the
Qian Long emperor**, has been excavated and is open to visitors.
This tomb is particularly worth visiting for its fine wall
carvings of Buddhist images in the emperor's coffin crypt.

These Buddhist images are unusual in imperial tomb architecture because of the contradictions in the ideologies of state Confucianism and Buddhism. Emperors were expected by more Confucian-minded ministers to keep religion at arm's length in the practice of imperial rituals. In the Ming period, ministers managed to prevent emperors from founding religious orders within the palace. However, Chinese Confucian civil servants had a harder job of enforcing state orthodoxy on their Manchu rulers who, like many other Central Asian and northern tribes people, had a tradition of Buddhist worship. The Qian Long emperor was an ardent Buddhist, despite his somewhat frequent veiled denials, and also believed that he, as emperor of China, was an incarnation of a bodhisattva, a Buddhist deity or saint. In addition to the Buddha images in the crypt there are Buddhist scriptures, or sutras, carved on the tomb walls in Tibetan and Sanskrit.

When the Xian Feng emperor died in Chengde in 1861, the crown prince, Tong Zhi was only a boy. Two women, the senior wife of the Xian Feng emperor and the mother of the new emperor, both became Empress Dowagers and were responsible for helping the boy to govern. The child emperor's mother, known to us in the West as the Empress Dowager and in Chinese as the *Ci Xi Tai Hou*, the Western Empress, was a shrewd and power-hungry character who managed to supplant her son and rule in his stead. Her counterpart, the *Ci An Tai Hou*, the Eastern Empress, was a kinder and milder figure and was unable to prevent imperial power from being stripped from the boy. Because of their equal status, the two empresses' tombs were built together in 1879 in two parallel enclosures. The tombs were built with identical buildings of modest dimensions but with roofs in the imperial yellow colour that befitted senior empresses. However, the Eastern Empress died first and the Western Empress Dowager then had her own part of the tomb rebuilt in 1895 with more lavish sacrificial halls constructed from *nan mu*. The **joint tombs of the two empresses** are known as *Ding Dong Ling* and a comparison of the two gives some idea of the scale of the Western Empress Dowager's extravagance and ambition. The carved ramp, or imperial carriageway, in front of her sacrificial hall, in the Qing tombs known as the **Profound Favour Hall**, *Long En Dian*, has the symbol of the empress, the phoenix, set *above* the symbol of the

A detail of the Manchu pigtail hairstyle on a statue of a civilian official at the subsidiary Spirit Avenue of the *Jing Ling*, tomb of the Kang Xi emperor, Eastern Qing Tombs.

The towerless, stone-walled mound at Mu Ling, tomb of the Dao Guang emperor, is unique amongst the imperial tombs of the Ming and Qing period. However, the plain tomb was not as inexpensive to build as it seems for the stone cladding required many different coloured fine stones which were quarried at great expense, Western Qing Tombs.

dragon, the emperor. The costly materials used in the buildings, the ornate latticework inside and outside the buildings, the presumptuous symbolism of the carvings and the sheer extravagance of decoration are undisguised statements of how the Western Empress Dowager viewed her supreme position.

As a last note on the Eastern Qing tombs, there are several details worth looking out for in the stone carvings. The first is in the Spirit Avenues. The Qing emperors were, in all matters, sticklers for the outward appearance of conformity to imperial tradition, and their Spirit Avenues follow the pattern set by the Ming emperors in all details except for the dress and hairstyle of the officials. Qing court costume was Manchu, as was the prescribed hairstyle of a shaved forehead and a long plait or queue (the Chinese always greatly resented the enforced loss of their own native male hairstyle of long hair dressed in a top knot). The stone figures of officials in the Qing Spirit Avenues depict Manchu dress and hairstyles, and some of the officials wear the rosary beads of Buddhism. These spirit avenue statues are very different from their Ming predecessors who are depicted in traditional Chinese court robes and hats. Note the stone memorial tablets housed in masonry pavilions before each tomb. These memorials bear inscriptions eulogizing the wisdom and achievements of the dead emperors. The stone tablets, or steles, are set on the backs of grotesque dragon-headed tortoises, who in ancient mythology were believed to hold the world on their backs. The tortoises stand on a square stone base carved to depict the sea. The sea is full of foaming waves and at each corner is a small whirlpool out of which appear a turtle, crab, prawn and a fish — all symbols of felicity.

Tour buses do make excursions to the Eastern Tombs and are worth joining up with if you are short of time. For those with more time and energy, it is recommended to make up a small group to hire a taxi in Peking and depart early in the morning for the Eastern Tombs, having agreed in advance with the driver a price for the day. Going by taxi allows you to visit the tombs at your own pace.

These tombs lie 120km (75 miles) to the west of Peking and now cover an area of 100km² (37.5 miles²). Four emperors are buried here: the Yong Zheng emperor (reigned 1723–35), at *Tai Ling*; the Jia Qing emperor (reigned 1796–1820), who died by lightning at Chengde, at *Chang Ling*; the Dao Guang emperor (reigned 1821–51), at *Mu Ling*; and the Guang Xu emperor (reigned 1875–1908), who initiated the failed Reform Movement of 1898 to overthrow the Empress Dowager, who is buried at *Chong Ling*.

THE WESTERN QING TOMBS — *XI LING*

The Western Tombs are currently being restored and, by all accounts, are in a beautiful, unspoilt setting. Visitors who wish to visit the tombs should try and contact a representative of China International Travel Service in their hotels before setting out, in order to find out the current status of the tombs. Travel by taxi is again recommended as the best means presently available of seeing the tombs.

View of the *Tai Ling*, the burial place of the Yong Zheng emperor, which is the initial and central tomb of the Western Qing Tombs.

147

THE GREAT WALL

The Great Wall of China dates back to the Warring States period of the Zhou dynasty (475–221 BC) when small states erected barriers against each other as well as to protect themselves from the non-Chinese tribes to the north. The first emperor of China, Qin Shi Huang Di (reigned 221–210 BC) linked up sections of the walls, and the succeeding Han dynasty (206 BC–AD 220) emperors continued this process to protect China against the Xiong Nu barbarians.

The Ming rulers, whose founding ancestor had driven the Mongol Yuan dynasty rulers back to their steppe homelands outside the Great Wall, put great store by the maintenance and rebuilding of the Wall, and most of the Great Wall we see today in north-east China dates from the Ming period (1368–1644) when the wall was extensively rebuilt in the 15th and 16th centuries.

But the Manchu Qing emperors who succeeded the Ming spent little time and money on the maintenance of the Great Wall, preferring instead to cement alliances with their nomadic neighbours with feasts and hunting expeditions held at their imperial resort at Chengde (see page 117). They believed that this was money better spent.

However, the Kang Xi emperor (reigned 1662–1722) understood the realities of the Great Wall more than most emperors.

> It is clear that, in order to hold the kingdom, the Emperor must exercise virtue and enable the people to feel contented. When the people are cheerfully submissive, the foundation of the empire has been laid, and the frontier is naturally secure . . . We have visited Gu Bei Kou and Xi Feng Kou [two strategic passes in the Great Wall] and we know that, in these places, most of the Wall is falling into ruins. If repairs are to be undertaken now, can it be done without injuring the people?
> From an edict of the Kang Xi emperor.

Kang Xi's nomadic ancestors had conquered China despite the lavish expenditure of the Ming emperors on the repair and

(Opposite) The Great Wall of China at Ba Da Ling.

149

extension of the Great Wall. For, after all, if the emperor himself is not able and just, his moral authority, and thus the loyalty of his subjects, is undermined. And, when an emperor and his authority are doubted by his people and his troops, no amount of masonry can save his dynasty. The troops of the Manchu army had broken through the Great Wall in 1644 with the complicity of Chinese generals of the Ming army who were disillusioned with their masters.

In the last 1,000 years of Chinese history, the country has had more than 600 years of rule by northern nomads. Two of the major dynasties of the last millenium, the Yuan (1276–1368) and Qing (1644–1912) were founded by nomadic tribal leaders who broke through the Great Wall to conquer and rule the whole of China.

Today, the various ancient and recent sections of the wall wind and loop across the mountains of North China and are estimated to add up to a total distance of 6,288km (3,930 miles) including all the truncated loops. There are 3,440km (2,150 miles) of continuous wall which extends from the north-east coast of China to the deserts of Central Asia. In the desert regions of Gansu province, it is possible to see the older sections of the wall which stand as eroded lines of compacted earth.

The Great Wall at *Ba Da Ling* and *Mu Tian Yu*, where most tours go, is spectacular because of its relentless route across the

Map of the Great Wall in the Ming period (1368–1644). Most of the north-eastern section of the Great Wall we can see today dates from this period.

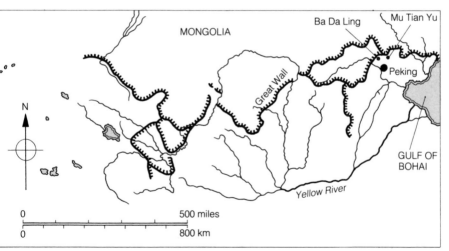

150

very peaks of the mountains. These are the Ming sections of the Great Wall and are built in stone and brick over an inner core of compacted earth and stones. Here the average height of the wall from its stone base to the crenellated parapets is 6–9m (20–30ft) with a width of 8m (25ft) at the base and 5m (16ft) at the top. In places, the inner core of the Wall has been reinforced with iron and wooden rods. At irregular intervals (irregular because the determining factor of siting was visibility between points) are watch towers in which troop concentrations were stationed. The watch towers of the Ming sections of the Wall have an average height of 12m (40ft) and a base width of 12m (40ft). Passes in the Wall were sited in narrow mountain valleys which were easy to defend.

There is a sad irony in the fact that the enduring architectural masterpiece of the Chinese imperial age is a monument to war and slave labour. The ancient glories of a civilization founded on the civil virtues of moral rectitude, learning and harmony between man and nature have long since vanished into the earth. We can only dream of the palaces of the Han, Tang and Song dynasties which were golden ages for native Chinese civilization. The savage magnificence of the Great Wall endures — a testimony in stone to the harsher realities of Chinese history.

CHRONOLOGY

DYNASTIES

	BC
Shang dynasty	c. 1480–1050
Zhou dynasty	c. 1122–221
(Warring States Period	475–221)
Qin dynasty	221–206
Han dynasty	206–AD 220

	AD
Wei, Jin, Northern and	
Southern dynasties	220–581
Sui dynasty	581–618
Tang dynasty	618–907
Five Dynasties and	
Ten kingdoms, including:	907–59
Liao dynasty in North China	907–1125
Song dynasty, including:	960–1279
Northern Song dynasty	960–1127
Southern Song dynasty	1127–1279
Jin dynasty in North China	1125–1234
Yuan dynasty	1276–1368
Ming dynasty	1368–1644
Qing dynasty	1644–1912

(The emperor was deposed in 1911 and formally abdicated in 1912.)

EMPERORS

MING EMPERORS

reign title		dates of reign	born
Hong Wu		1368–98	1328
Jian Wen		1399–1402	1377
Yong Le		1402–24	1360
Hong Xi		1425	1378
Xuan De		1426–35	1399
Zheng Tong		1436–49	1427
Jing Tai	same emperor deposed and restored, two reign titles	1450–57	1428
Tian Xun		1457–64	1428
Cheng Hua		1465–87	1447

Hong Zhi	1488–1505	1470
Zheng De	1506–21	1491
Jia Jing	1522–66	1507
Long Qing	1567–72	1537
Wan Li	1573–1620	1563
Tai Chang	1620	1582
Tian Qi	1621–27	1605
Chong Zhen	1628–44	1611

PRE-CONQUEST MANCHU OVERLORDS	*dates of reign (in Shenyang)*	*born*
Nurhaci	1583–1626	1559
Abahai	1626–43	1592

QING EMPERORS

reign title	*dates of reign*	*born*
Shun Zhi	1644–61	1638
Kang Xi	1662–1722	1654
Yong Zheng	1723–35	1678
Qian Long	1736–95	1711
Jia Qing	1796–1820	1760
Dao Guang	1821–50	1782
Xian Feng	1851–61	1831
Tong Zhi	1862–74	1856
Guang Xu	1875–1908*	1871
Xuan Tong (Henry Pu Yi)	1909–12	1906

* During Guang Xu reign, the Empress Dowager, Ci Xi Tai Hou, was Regent from 1889–98, and continued to wield power until her death in 1908.

GLOSSARY

Chinese Terms

Ang a bird-beak-shaped, diagonally slanted, lever arm. Load-bearing in early architecture but of decorative value in late Ming and Qing periods.

Chi wen an acroterion in the form of a large ceramic tile placed at either end of roof ridge. Normally dragon-headed, but early versions were fish tail-shaped. It had the practical function of protecting wooden nails holding tiles of roof ridge.

Dian a formal hall.

Dou gong bracket set; series of bracket blocks and arms designed to distribute weight of roof on supporting columns.

Feng shui literally 'wind and water'; the traditional science of geomancy used for siting buildings and tombs.

Gong a palace hall.

He xi palace or formal imperial style of paint decoration on wood work of buildings, featuring dragon and geometric designs.

Jian a bay; the distance between two main columns in a building, used as a unit of measure.

Lou a building of more than one storey.

Men a gate.

Su shi ornamental or Suzhou-style of the paint decoration on woodwork of buildings in gardens, featuring images of landscapes, birds and flowers etc.

Ta stupa or dagoba; a structure of varying shape and size which was originally designed to hold Buddhist sacred relics, texts, or the remains of a venerated monk.

Ting a garden pavilion of varying shape and size.

Xie a water-side or hill-view garden pavilion.

Yin and *Yang* the names of the female and male elements seen as inherent in all creation. Yin is the female, watery and dark; yang is male, light and sunny. Yin numbers are odd; yang numbers are even.

Chinese Emblems and Symbols

Painted and carved motifs commonly seen in Chinese architecture:

Eight Buddhist symbols: wheel; conch shell; umbrella; canopy; lotus; vase; pair of fishes; eternal knot.

Eight precious objects: jewel; cash; open lozenge; solid lozenge; musical stone; pair of books; pair of horns; artemisia leaf.
(Seen, for example, at the base of stone altars and columns in tomb architecture.)

Emblem flowers: peony, the flower of spring; lotus, the flower of summer; chrysanthemum, the flower of autumn; camellia, the flower of winter

Mythological animals:

Crane emblem of longevity. Associated with immortals who have achieved their immortality through study and meditation on earth.

Dragon the most important and powerful

154

emblem in imperial art. The dragon is male and lives within the watery elements of clouds, rivers and lakes. He brings water to the land and is invoked for good harvests. The five-clawed dragon is the symbol of the emperor.

Lion   guardian lions, set in pairs outside the main entrances in Chinese buildings, symbolize the power and authority of the occupant.

Phoenix   came to symbolize the Empress in late imperial times.

Qi lin   a mythological animal often referred to in English as a unicorn, but in Chinese is depicted as both one- and two-horned. It has hooves, a scaly body and bulging eyes.

Tortoise   an emblem of longevity and strength, and thus carries memorial tables, or stelae, on its back.

Xie zhi   a mythological animal with a strong resemblance to a lion; believed to be able to judge good and evil in men.

Symbolism of colours in imperial times:
Green   the east and spring.
Red   the south and summer; also the colour of good fortune and weddings.
Yellow   the centre; also the colour of the Emperor. No private citizen could use yellow in apparel or architecture.
White   the west and autumn; also the colour of mourning and death.
Black   the north and winter.

BIBLIOGRAPHY

Historical Background

Dawson, Raymond, *The Chinese Experience*, New York, 1978

Huang, Ray, *1587 A Year of No Significance*, Yale, 1981

Hucker, Charles, *The Ming Dynasty: Its Origins and Evolving Institutions*, Michigan, 1978

Fairbank, John K. & Twitchett, Denis (eds), *The Cambridge History of China*, Vol. 7 Part 1, Vol. 10 Part 1, Vol. 11 Part 2, Cambridge, 1979

Wakeman, Frederic, *The Great Enterprise*, Vol. 1, California, 1985

Architectural History and Arts

Blaser, Werner, *Chinese Pavilion Architecture*, Niederteufen, Switzerland, 1974

Boerschman, Ernest, *Chinese Architecture and its Relation to Chinese Culture*, Annual Report of the Smithsonian Institute, Washington, 1911

Boyd, Andrew, *Chinese Architecture*, London, 1962

Cheng Da Liu, *The Great Wall of China*, Hong Kong, 1984

Chung Wah Nan, *The Art of Chinese Gardens*, Hong Kong, 1982

Eberhard, Wolfram, *A Dictionary of Chinese Symbols*, London, 1986

Fairbank, Wilma (ed.), *A Pictorial History of Chinese Architecture* by Liang Ssu-cheng, Boston, 1984

Hardie, Alison (transl.), *The Craft of Gardens* by Ji Cheng, Yale, 1988

Keswick, Maggie, *The Chinese Garden: History, Art & Architecture*, London, 1986

Luo Ze Wen, *The Great Wall*, London, 1982

Malone, Carroll Brown, *Summer Palaces of the Ch'ing Dynasty*, New York, 1966

Needham, Joseph, *Science and Civilisation in China*, Vol. 4.3, Cambridge, 1971

Paludan, Ann, *The Imperial Ming Tombs*, Yale, 1981

Pirazolli-T'Serstevens, Michèle, *Living Architecture: Chinese*, London 1972

Sirén, Osvald, *Les Palais Impériaux de Pékin*, Paris, 1926, *Gardens of China*, New York, 1949

Steinhardt, Nancy Shatzman, *Chinese Traditional Architecture*, New York, 1984

Sullivan, Michael, *The Arts of China*, California, 1967

Tregear, Mary, *Chinese Art*, London 1980

Geomancy, Cosmology and Philosophy

Bennett, Steven J., 'Patterns of the Sky and Earth: A Chinese Science of Applied Cosmology', in the journal *Chinese Science*, Philadelphia, March 1978

Henderson, John B., *The Development and Decline of Chinese Cosmology*, New York, 1984

March, Andrew, 'An Appreciation of Chinese Geomancy' in the *Journal of Asian Studies*, Vol. 27 no. 2, New York, 1968

Meyer, Jeffrey F., 'Peking as a Sacred City' in the journal *Asian Folklore & Social Life Monographs*, Vol. 81, Taipei, 1976, 'Feng Shui of the Chinese City' in the journal *History of Religions*, Chicago, Nov 1978

Schwartz, Benjamin, *The World of Chinese Thought in Ancient China*, Harvard, 1985

Reference Works and General Guides

Arlington, Lewis Charles & Lewisohn, William, *In Search of Old Peking*, New York, 1967

Chan, Charis, *The Collins Illustrated Guide to All China*, London, 1988

Geil, William Edgar, *The Great Wall of China*, London, 1909

Hedin, Sven, *Jehol City of Emperors*, London, 1932

Hook, Brian (ed.), *The Cambridge Encyclopedia-Guide of China*, Cambridge, 1982

Johnston, Reginald, *Twilight in the Forbidden City*, Oxford, 1985

Nagel's Encyclopedia-Guide China, Geneva, 1973

Wan Yi, *Daily Life in the Forbidden City*, Harmondsworth, 1988

ACKNOWLEDGEMENTS

Photographs
Ancient Art and Architecture Collection/D. Harrison: p. 103; Heather Angel: p. 73 (bottom); Bibliotheque Nationale: p. 104; Philip Bingham: pp. 57, 69; British Library: pp. 5, 9 (top), 16, 40; Courtesy of the Trustees of the British Museum: pp. 1, 20, 21, 23; Sharon Bishop: p. 2; J. Allan Cash Photo Library: jacket photograph and pp. 22, 38, 56, 60, 100; Douglas Dickins: pp. 52, 58, 59, 72, 91, 92; Musée Guimet © Photo R.M.N.: pp. 54, 118; Sally and Richard Greenhill: p. 90; Tom Hanley: p. 148; Jimmy Holmes: pp. 36, 63, 98; MacQuitty International Collection: p. 64; Ann Paludan: pp. 12, 13, 30, 35, 49, 50 (bottom), 51 (top), 115, 128 (top), 132, 135, 138, 139, 142, 143, 146, 147; Graham de Smidt: pp. 50 (top), 65, 68, 82, 83, 86, 127, 128 (bottom), 129, 130, 131; François Ward: pp. 51 (bottom), 62, 67, 73 (top), 77, 80, 94, 99, 111, 112, 113, 116, 123, 124, 125; Wellcome Institute Library London: p. 9 (bottom); Werner Forman Archive: pp. xi, 55.

Plans
The following sources have provided the basis for certain maps and plans in this book and the author and publishers acknowledge with gratitude permission from the relevant copyright-holders for this use.

The No. 1 China Historical Research Academy, from *The Imperial Mausoleums of the Qing Dynasty*, 1982,: p. vii; The Chinese Architectural and Construction Press from *The History of Classical Chinese Architecture*, 2nd edit. 1978: pp. 19, 37, 44, 47, 74, 88, 141; The Science Press, Beijing, from *History and Development of Ancient Chinese Architecture*, 1986,: p. 21; Birkhauser Verlag AG, Basel, from *Courtyard Houses in China: Tradition and Present* by Werner Blaser: p. 25; China House Gallery, from *Chinese Traditional Architecture* by Nancy Shatzman Steinhardt, 1984: p. 27; Alec Tirant, London, from *Chinese Architecture* by Andrew Boyd, 1962 (borrowed from Liang Ssu-ch'eng ed. Wilma Fairbank – see below): p. 28; Penguin Books Ltd. from *Chinese Art* by W. Willetts Vol. 2.: p. 29; MIT from *A Pictorial History of Chinese Architecture* by Liang Ssu-ch'eng, (ed. Wilma Fairbank) Boston, 1984: p. 32, 33, 34; Commercial Press, Hong Kong, from *Palaces of the Forbidden City*, 1982 (ed. Yu Zhuoyun): p. 70; Zhaohua Publishing House, Peking, from *Summer Palace*, 1981: p. 105; *The Imperial Ming Tombs* by Ann Paludan, Yale, 1981: p. 137; *Living Architecture: Chinese*. by Michele Pirazolli-T'Serstevens, London, 1972: p. 150.

Every effort has been made to trace copyright-holders; it is hoped that any omission will be excused.

INDEX

INDEX

INDEX

INDEX